THE RURAL INDUSTRIES
OF ENGLAND & WALES

III
DECORATIVE CRAFTS
AND RURAL POTTERIES

THE SPINNER

Reproduced by kind permission of Mrs. Mairet

THE RURAL INDUSTRIES
OF ENGLAND & WALES

A SURVEY MADE ON BEHALF OF THE
AGRICULTURAL ECONOMICS
RESEARCH INSTITUTE
OXFORD

III
DECORATIVE CRAFTS
AND RURAL POTTERIES

By
HELEN E. FITZRANDOLPH
and M. DORIEL HAY

EP Publishing Limited
1978

First published Oxford University Press, 1927

Republished 1978 by
EP Publishing Limited
East Ardsley, Wakefield
West Yorkshire, England

Copyright © 1978 Oxford University Press

ISBN 0 7158 1255 6

British Library Cataloguing in Publication Data
FitzRandolph, Helen E
  The rural industries of England & Wales.
  3: Decorative crafts and rural potteries.
  1. England – Rural conditions
  2. England – Industries – History – 20th century
  I. Title II. Hay, M Doriel III. Jones, A M
  IV. University of Oxford. Agricultural Economics
  Research Institute
  338'.0942   HC256.3
  ISBN 0-7158-1255-6

Please address all enquiries to EP Publishing Limited
(address as above)

Printed in Great Britain by
The Scolar Press Limited
Ilkley, West Yorkshire

PREFACE

In any consideration of the development of the country-side the place and function of local industries in rural life must occupy a prominent position. Their importance in the past is obvious, when the village was largely an isolated economic unit ; in view of the part they might still play in maintaining a fuller life for the country dweller, in stemming the flow of population from the rural to the urban centres, and in solving some of the problems of modern industrialism, the need for a study of their present state, of the extent to which the changes in modern, social, and economic conditions demand their supersession, and of the possibility of adapting and developing them to serve these same conditions, becomes increasingly apparent.

It may be that rural industries can continue to supplement agriculture in the complete rural community, by providing subsidiary employment for the part-time land-worker and the small-holder ; by affording the chance of employment in their own homes or villages to the various members of their families ; by providing certain requisites of agricultural industry. It may be possible that in the revolution of economic principles and systems which is now being made by all sorts and conditions of persons, certain human advantages in rural industries may be set against the greater production of goods by the larger industrial units of the towns. In particular, the smaller industrial concern enables a man to see the whole series of connexions between the making and using of an article, and brings his work into direct relation not only with his own life, but with that of the community of which he is a member. There is little or no distinction between producer and consumer, and one of the chief causes of present social conflicts is non-existent. The worker in the country ' sees the nature of what he is doing ; he is getting products from the land and making use of them by industry. He sees the whole process, and the fact is plain that labour and land are for the sake of himself and others

like him who needs the goods. He sees the grain become
flour, the wood from the forest become furniture, the hide
become leather, and the leather boots, and the wool cloth—
all beside him, and all of it a plain process of natural goods
made useful by men.' ¹ The men of the towns, however,
have a genius for organization, and if it be necessary that
their business should be arranged on a basis involving less
specialization than at present, or so that some of the evil
effects of over-specialization were eliminated, they may be
able to modify existing systems without seriously affecting
their productivity. The only basis upon which rural industries can be firmly established is that of a high standard
of technical knowledge and skill, suitable machinery, and
commercial organization. On the other hand, the moribund
condition of many once-flourishing country trades and crafts
may have to be recognized as the price of industrial progress
in other centres. The modern tendency towards the centrali-
zation of industry and large-scale production ; the enormous
development of transport facilities which has broken down
the barriers between town and country ; the danger of these
small unorganized enterprises becoming sweated industries
serving only to subsidize agricultural wages, all of these things
may render undesirable any effort towards the resuscitation
of many of these ancient crafts.

With so little knowledge available it became clear that
a thorough investigation of the position of rural industries,
both economic and social, would be advantageous and, in
1919, at the suggestion of the Development Commissioners,
an inquiry into the condition of rural industries in the neighbourhood of Oxford was set on foot by the Agricultural
Economics Research Institute, at Oxford. It was rather
of the nature of a trial trip, an experimental inquiry to
explore the possibilities of a more complete investigation, and
in the following year arrangements were made with the
Development Commissioners and the Ministry of Agriculture
for an extension of the survey so as to bring under review
the principal rural industries of England and Wales.

¹ D. H. Macgregor, *The Evolution of Industry*, p. 24.

The terms of reference of those responsible for the work were to consider—

(1) the existing rural industries and the causes of their establishment in particular localities, such as easy access to local supplies of raw material and labour, and local markets for the finished products ;

(2) the various types of organization in these industries, such as small factories and workrooms or individual production, organizations for the purchase of raw materials or the sale of finished products. Educational facilities and the possibilities of technical instruction were also to be borne in mind in this connexion ;

(3) the economic and social effects of rural industries, the conditions of labour attendant on them, the connexion between rural industries and agricultural employment, and how far such industries tend to depress or to ameliorate the lot of the agricultural worker ;

(4) the prospects of development of existing industries and of the introduction of new enterprises, or of the resuscitation of former industries now dead or in a state of suspended animation. In this connexion the existence of competition, both urban and foreign, was to be borne in mind, and consideration given to the conditions under which rural industries can compete with urban production.

The survey was carried out during three years by a specially appointed group of workers. They surveyed the country, county by county, and the results of their inquiries were embodied in reports dealing with the industries of particular localities. From these interim reports (which are available in manuscript, for consultation, at Oxford) the final reports were compiled, dealing with the various industries separately as they occur throughout the country.

As has already been said, the first district surveyed was that of Oxfordshire, and the investigator in this instance was Miss K. S. Woods, who was assisted in part of the work by Miss C. D. Biggs. The results of the survey were embodied in book form, and published early in 1921.[1] From

[1] K. S. Woods, *Rural Industries Round Oxford* (Oxford University Press).

1921 to 1922 the work was continued by Miss Woods and Miss Helen FitzRandolph, and in the summer of 1922 Miss M. Doriel Hay took Miss Woods's place. The survey of the Welsh industries required a knowledge of the Welsh language and was undertaken, apart from the English survey, by Miss A. M. Jones, in 1922 and 1923. All these investigators worked under the direction of Mr. A. W. Ashby. A list of the districts surveyed by each is appended.

The investigators must be congratulated upon the results of their work. Inquiries of this kind are not always too easily conducted, and call for a measure of enthusiasm and even of courage in those concerned if the best results are to be obtained.

It is impossible to name all those who assisted them in their work, but I should like to make grateful acknowledgement of the friendly reception accorded to them, and of the readiness with which those engaged in the various industries investigated gave of their time and knowledge. Without their cordial co-operation it would have been an impossible task.

For convenience of publication the reports have been collected together in four volumes, as follows :

Vol. I. Timber and Underwood Industries and some Village Workshops.

Vol. II. Osier Growing and Basketry, and Some Rural Factories.

Vol. III. Decorative Crafts and Rural Potteries.

Vol. IV. Rural Industries in Wales.

The following report is Vol. III of the series. The industries with which it deals are largely those which have been developed by the Women's Institute movement and by similar social organizations, and considerable progress has been made in some of the handicrafts described since the date of their investigation. But reviewing this growth nothing seems to have occurred to necessitate any revision of the general conclusions drawn by the investigators three years ago.

C. S. ORWIN.

AGRICULTURAL ECONOMICS
RESEARCH INSTITUTE,
OXFORD, *November 1926.*

ORDER OF THE SURVEY

Date.	District.	Investigator.
1919–20	Oxfordshire	K. S. Woods and C. D. Biggs
1920–1	Bedfordshire	Helen FitzRandolph
1921	Derbyshire, Leicestershire, and Notting-hamshire	,,
1921–2	Kent, Surrey, and Sussex	,,
,,	Westmorland, Cumberland, and Lanca-shire	,,
1922	Shropshire, Staffordshire, and Cheshire	K. S. Woods
,,	Herefordshire and Worcestershire	,,
,,	South Western Counties	,,
,,	Durham	Helen FitzRandolph
,,	Northumberland	,,
,,	North Riding of Yorkshire	Helen FitzRandolph and M. Doriel Hay
,,	East and West Ridings of Yorkshire	M. Doriel Hay
,,	Carnarvonshire	A. M. Jones
,,	Denbighshire	,,
,,	Flint	,,
1923	Gloucestershire	Helen FitzRandolph
,,	East Anglia and Essex	,,
,,	Lincolnshire	M. Doriel Hay
,,	Warwickshire	,,
,,	East Midland Counties	,,
,,	Merionethshire and Montgomeryshire	A. M. Jones
,,	Brecon and Radnorshire	,,
,,	Pembrokeshire, Cardiganshire, Carmar-thenshire, and Anglesey	,,
,,	Monmouthshire and Glamorganshire	,,

CONTENTS

ILLUSTRATIONS

CHAPTER I

INTRODUCTORY

DECORATIVE CRAFTS AND THEIR PLACE IN VILLAGE LIFE

THE craft-work and industries dealt with in this volume are miscellaneous and are carried on by many different types of people with various aims. The point which they have in common and which makes it possible to group them together and speak of the conditions and prospects of the whole group, is that they are all concerned mainly with the production of decorative work. They do not supply the demands of *local* groups of people, their customers being linked together by a certain community of taste though often widely scattered throughout England. These industries produce not so much the mere necessities of life as its ornaments. This may seem to be perilously near to the point of view, so distressing to the genuine craftsman, that 'art' is something which is ornamental but useless, and that use and decoration have no connexion. No confusion of this kind is intended, but it is an undeniable fact that in nearly every case a hand-made article costs more than the factory-made equivalent. The customer who can afford the greater outlay and who appreciates craftsmanship sufficiently to do so, obtains value not only in individuality of design but also in durability or strength, the results of good workmanship. But it is by virtue of its decorative quality that the hand-made article—the product of the industries described here—is more attractive to the customer than the factory-made article. The greater number of the general public, however, is inclined to follow the line of least resistance ; therefore not only is the average customer more likely to enter any of the hundred shops selling factory goods than to seek out the one selling handicraft work, but, moreover, from dread of appearing to be eccentric, will prefer articles of stereotyped design rather than trust to his own taste in choosing something unusual. It would be absurd to deny that any factory products are beautiful, but because the factory system involves the production of a great number of articles on exactly the same pattern, the aim of the factory designer must be to create something which will satisfy the needs of the greatest possible number of people, except in the case of goods of the most expensive kind. The handicraft worker's asset is that he can express his own individuality by producing things for the taste of individual customers.

With the great improvements which are continually being made in all kinds of machinery, the generalization that factory products are necessarily inferior in durability to craft-work is no longer true, although practical utility, fitness, and strength are characteristics of all good craftsmanship. The workman shaping his material with his hands, or with tools directed by his hands, can adapt his work more exactly to the natural idiosyncrasies of the material than is possible with a machine. Hand-spun and hand-woven material coloured with vegetable dyes will, if well made, be at least equally, and in many cases more, durable as compared with machine-made fabric at the same cost. Hand-work gives to a piece of lace or of pottery certain utilitarian qualities in addition to the distinction of beauty. Cheap household crockery will crack and crumble in a way that the more expensive hand-thrown ware, of more carefully welded clay, would never do. It is interesting to notice in this connexion that the common flower-pot is one of the few things in every-day use which, like baskets, must still be made by hand, no satisfactory machine-made substitute having been discovered.

It remains true, however, that the greater initial outlay on hand-made things is impossible for many purchasers, and therefore the work of the decorative craft industries can perhaps be described as hand-work for those who are able and willing to pay for beauty and craftsmanship in things of everyday use which could be bought more cheaply if stereotyped factory products were chosen. A study of the work of the small rural potteries shows that it is not only in such things as fabrics and lace, in which appearance is obviously of importance, that craftsmanship is still worth while. It is true that many of those potteries which made ' brown ware ' for household use have recently died out, owing to the increasing popularity of cheap enamelled iron utensils and to the gradual extinction of certain branches of housecraft ; thus there is little demand now for the big pans in which pies and bread were baked at home, the use of separators is rendering obsolete the wide bowls in which milk was set for the cream to rise, and there is less sale for the jars in which eggs were preserved by the careful house-wife. Nevertheless, some of these small potteries in which this pleasant old-fashioned ware is still hand-thrown—a

method which gives a well-balanced shape and a well-made
pot—are still flourishing and continue to find a steady market
for their ware.

Of the various groups of craft-work considered in this
volume, jet and serpentine working is perhaps in the lowest
grade artistically and the generalizations set out in this introduction apply less to these than to the other crafts.   The
serpentine work dates from about seventy years ago, having
been started at a period when commercial industrialism was
at its height and artistic appreciation at its lowest.   Jet
working is of very ancient origin, but during the last hundred
years at least, it has developed on lines similar to those of
the serpentine industry, most of the work being done to
supply cheap jewellery shops, where it is sold as ' souvenirs '
to visitors.   In the case of serpentine there seems to be some
scope for the development of the industry on better lines by
turning the real beauty of colour and grain in the marble to
worthier account.

The pottery industry is, of those considered here, the
oldest as a general rural industry, and the small country
potteries show signs of development on lines quite different
from those of the big industrial firms of Staffordshire.
Pottery work is also becoming popular in the ' arts and crafts '
movement, and useful experiments in the use of local clay
and of simple glazes and in improved methods of firing
result from this.   The small rural pottery seems to have a
definite future as one of the decorative craft industries, in
addition to the survival of the humbler, but no less worthy,
potteries producing simple household ware and flower-pots.

The hand-weaving and spinning industries had become
almost extinct as cottage crafts before they were revived in
the nineteenth century and they are therefore being developed
rather on the lines of a new handicraft than as one of the older
types of rural industry.   The tradition behind these crafts,
however, keeps them in touch with actual village life, and
the possibility of the use of local raw materials—of fleeces
from the flocks of the district and of lichens and plants for
dyes—helps to relate them to local conditions.   Thus, they
are of particular interest from the point of view of this survey.
In the same way the rural potteries, which in many cases
make use of local clays, have in this respect more in common
with the other traditional village crafts than have many of
the newer handicraft enterprises.

Lace-making is a genuine old cottage industry, still carried
out on traditional lines, although to a much smaller extent

than formerly. In this case attempts are being made by the arts and crafts movement to keep the industry alive, but, owing to many difficulties peculiar to this craft, for example the immense amount of time which must go to the making of a yard even of the simplest lace, together with the real beauty of the machine-made substitute at a very much lower cost, the prospects for the revival or further development of this craft in its present form are doubtful.

The chapter on ' Home Crafts and Industries ' includes a great many different types of craft-work done under various circumstances. None of the main currents of the recognized commercial industries are dealt with here, although in some instances a craft is considered which is akin to the ordinary trades. Thus a few makers of cane baskets are included who have little connexion with the main basket-making industry. Their training has been different from that of the regular basket-maker, and their wares are of a type differing from any of the standard commercial patterns, and are sold through other channels. The glove-making carried on by members of Women's Institutes is also treated here because the organization of this home industry is on entirely different lines from that of the commercial glove trade.

The ' Home Crafts and Industries ' include work done in connexion with organizations such as the Home Arts and Industries Association and the Women's Institutes which are not commercial bodies but are concerned with some aspect of the encouragement of craft-work for the sake of its educational value. They do not include the out-workers for factories, who are dealt with elsewhere.[1] They include whole- or part-time work done by persons not otherwise employed in ordinary trades and also by those who, working at a trade for their livelihood, engage in handicraft work in their spare time for recreation rather than for the sake of the financial return, although the latter may be of value to them. Examples of the former class of workers are persons with a small fixed income who need to add to this but can afford to choose an occupation which is more congenial and interesting than remunerative. Amongst these workers there are many women who can practise a handicraft in the time spared from their household duties. In the latter category are the evening classes for metal-work which are organized for boys and men engaged in farm work during the day. This

[1] See vol. ii, *Osier Growing, Basketry Industries and Some Rural Factories,* Part I, Chapter III, ' Outwork for Factories '.

particular craft of metal-work is generally carried on in a workshop, but as a rule the home industries, as their name implies, are of such a simple type, needing no elaborate tools or apparatus and no machinery, that they can be carried on in the workers' homes.

Some of the new enterprises are being built up on the foundations of old indigenous crafts, as in the case of rush-plaiting, revived in certain districts by Women's Institute workers, and the quilting in traditional patterns which is done by the countrywomen of Northumberland and other northern counties.

Many of these workers in home crafts, like many of the hand-loom weavers and some potters, are artists whose enterprises cannot be developed on an extensive scale owing to the very nature of the work, which owes much of its value to its personal character. An individual artist, working alone, is of no particular significance from the point of view of a survey of rural industries unless his work has some especial influence upon or relation to the district, or unless he trains country people as apprentices to his craft, and so really founds an industry, not merely an individual enterprise which has no chance of surviving him. Individual workers or small groups of workers are therefore important from the point of view of this survey in so far as they represent the movement to combat the ill effects of industrialism by keeping alive in the country a knowledge of and interest in hand-work, and by preserving from extinction the traditional skill of English craftsmen. Many artist craftsmen affirm that talent and capacity for original design can more easily be awakened in country people, who have not felt the deadening effects of industrialism, than in townspeople.

From the educational and social aspects also the handicraft work of rural districts is interesting, for such work forms part of nearly all schemes for the improvement of village life. The economic value of the work may be small in comparison with that of large industries, but to many individuals it is considerable. Although many of these industries and home crafts have little relation to local conditions in so far as raw materials or the marketing of finished goods is concerned, yet in so much as they help to provide a new occupation and source of livelihood, particularly for the young people of the villages, they are of local importance. Moreover, certain points in connexion with these crafts have a bearing on the vital question of apprenticeship and training in more important industries.

Since the products of most of the industries dealt with
here do not, as has been pointed out, supply the demands
of any local groups of people in the same way in which, for
example, the hurdle-maker, wheelwright, or basket-maker
works for neighbouring farmers and tradesmen, the marketing problems connected with the industries described in this
survey are somewhat different from those of the other rural
industries.   Many of the older village craftsmen, however,
are finding the necessity of seeking a wider market, as their
former customers turn, for certain goods, to factory-made
products.   The 'handicraft' workers have found special
methods of marketing necessary owing to the individual
character of their goods and the fact that their output, being
largely unorganized and often the product only of spare-
time work, is small and somewhat erratic.   Their system of
displaying their wares at exhibitions and otherwise making
them more widely known, of obtaining orders, and getting
into personal touch with their customers, is one in which
they might sometimes co-operate with the workers in the
older village industries to the advantage of both.   The
possibilities of this method of marketing, even for the older
and more purely utilitarian industries, have been demonstrated by a certain firm which is building up a successful
business by getting into touch with such rural craftsmen as
makers of wattle goods and baskets, who cannot find a local
outlet for their work.   This firm arranges exhibits of these
products at agricultural shows and obtains orders from
different parts of the country which are passed on to the
village workers to be executed.

In these chapters some attempt is made, in giving an
account of the 'decorative crafts', to indicate the extent
of the movement which encourages them, their possible
future, and the direction in which further developments,
particularly in organization, education, and technical training, are likely to tend.   Finally, in summing up the general
situation and prospects of each industry or group of crafts,
the aim has been to define its value to village men and women,
a value which depends mainly upon its relation to local
conditions—economic and social—and upon the extent to
which it meets their interests and needs.

CHAPTER II

HAND-LOOM WEAVING, DYEING, AND SPINNING

i. *Distribution of the Weaving Industries.*

THE hand-loom weaving industries which exist in England are of two main types, being either a survival of an old indigenous industry or else of comparatively recent origin, having been founded within the last twenty or thirty years, and in many cases since the war. The majority of these newer industries are carried on by people of the better educated (and generally considered ' leisured ') classes, who have been attracted by the artistic possibilities of the craft of weaving. Hand-loom weaving has become a popular hobby amongst those who can afford the necessary outlay on the apparatus, and who have space in which to set up a loom, as well as enough of the genuine craftsman's capacity for taking pains. These weavers often find that their hobby can be developed to a profitable part-time occupation, and thus under the heading of hand-loom weaving are to be found many activities which it is difficult to distinguish either as hobbies or industries, partaking, as they do, of the nature of both. As there are also to be considered the workshops organized on commercial lines, in which are sometimes a number of employees, the industry as a whole cannot be included under the heading of ' Home Crafts '. (See Chapter IV.)

Traces of weaving industries of ancient origin are still to be found in Somerset and Wiltshire, in Northumberland, around Coventry, near Canterbury, at North Lopham in Norfolk, and in connexion with the big silk-weaving industry at Sudbury and Haverhill in Suffolk, and Braintree in Essex. Another survival of hand-loom weaving is to be found in every textile factory, a few hand-weavers being employed to weave short pieces of every new pattern, which can be sent out as specimens of the material which is to be made.

Weaving industries of more recent origin flourish in two important groups, one situated in the Lake District, the other in Sussex, and also in many workshops scattered throughout other counties. The hand-loom weaving of the

Lake District originated in an attempt to revive the old industry, which still existed there until quite recently as a traditional craft in many farm-houses. This survival of hand-loom weaving in a few districts is to be accounted for chiefly by the existence of some particular demand which can only be supplied by the hand-loom, or else by the connexion of the industry with a circle of old-fashioned customers who have been slow to accept factory-made goods.

Locally grown flax and hemp were woven on hand-looms in many Somerset villages into linen and sail-cloth. At East Coker, near Yeovil, there are old people still living who worked on the ' pair of looms ', as the loom was called. In old times the farmer and his family would carry through all the processes, from the sowing of the flax to the weaving of the ' web ', but the spinning became a factory process long before power-looms had taken the bulk of the weaving trade, and the spinning mills of Crewkerne (Somerset) and of Bridport (Dorset) and Coker (Wilts.) continued to supply the cottage weavers with yarn. In several villages of Somerset there are now mills making sail-cloth, matting, and webbing, as well as rope and twine, but no use is made of locally grown flax and only mechanical processes are employed, so this industry is no longer a rural one.

The Wilton carpet factories, although from the point of view of organization they belong rather to the group of rural factories [1] than to the hand-weaving industries, should be mentioned here because they are closely connected with other relics of the ancient textile industries of Wiltshire. The factory at Wilton itself is a very large one, sixty girls being employed at the hand-looms making patterned carpets, whilst plain ones are woven on power-looms, worked by men. There are four smaller branch factories for hand-weaving at the villages of Tisbury, Mere, Downton, and Fordingbridge.

Although the modern sail-cloth and woollen textile mills have little direct connexion with the village weavers of former times, there are still a few weaving sheds in which the old traditions are being handed on to a younger generation of weavers or, rather, had been handed on and were kept alive until a few years ago, for two of these sheds were already closed when visited in 1921. One of these was at Winterslow, near Salisbury, and was set up fifty years ago by a lady interested in the revival of rural industries for the use of the small-holders settled there. She had organized the

[1] See vol. ii, *Osier Growing, Basketry Industries and Some Rural Factories.*

industry for some years and later it had passed into the hands of the weavers themselves. After the war about ten ex-service men had received a nine-months course of training here, but, when the place was visited, they had all dispersed and the weaver who had instructed them had also left the neighbourhood. The Government training scheme seems to have been a failure and in the master-weaver's own home, where he had several looms, all standing idle, there were stocks of tweed which could not be disposed of. The failure of this enterprise may possibly have been due to a lack of business experience on the part of the craftsmen. The materials made were good and serviceable tweeds for country wear, for which there should have been a ready sale. Another hand-weaving and spinning industry, which used to employ one man weaver and thirty-five women and girls spinning, had come to an end during the war, when the weaver went away to take up war-work and the spinners found other employment. Early in 1921 there were again two weavers at work, although only on part time, and a shop had been opened to sell the tweed which was made.

Woollen materials are still hand-woven in a few mills in Northumberland villages. At Tossen, near Rothbury, there is a rather languishing industry which has a very antiquated air. A spinning jenny of primitive pattern was installed there long ago, but the water-power which worked it having been cut off for the supply of a town, the wool is now sent to another mill to be spun and returns to Tossen to be woven on the ancient looms. In a larger and very flourishing business at Otterburn several hand-looms are still in use for the weaving of plaid travelling rugs.

In a group of industrial villages between Coventry and Nuneaton there is some survival of the once famous and prosperous industry of weaving ribbons on hand-looms. The work is now carried on as outwork for Coventry factories and the organization and extent of the industry are therefore described in another volume.[1]

Canterbury has been a centre of the weaving industry since the refugee Huguenot weavers settled there in the seventeenth century, and there is a tradition to the effect that the earlier Flemish refugees also plied their craft in this city. An old building standing in a garden on the river Stour is pointed out as the one in which these weavers from the Netherlands set up their looms, and, by a coincidence,

[1] Vol. ii, *Osier Growing, Basketry Industries and Some Rural Factories*, Part I, Chapter III, ' Outwork for Factories '.

it was in this same house that some of the Belgian refugees
were sheltered during the last war. Descendants of the
Huguenot weavers carried on a hand-spinning industry
outside Canterbury until a few years ago, although they now
only conduct a general drapery business. Another firm
continued until lately the weaving on hand-looms of sacking
for ' hop-pockets ' (the large sacks used for hops), ' sails ',
(canvas covers for hay-ricks), and linen for table use. Hand-
looms are now no longer in use by either of these firms.

At North Lopham, in Norfolk, there are still the relics of
a linen industry which, until it came to an end as a regular
business two years ago, had been carried on by many
generations of the same family. Four or five years ago there
were about a dozen weavers at work and seven or eight were
employed until the business was closed down. Now only
one old man, a gardener, does a little weaving in his spare
time during the winter for the lady who still owns the
business. Damask table linen, towels, and sheets were made
here and used to be sold through travellers and to a London
warehouse. There were two other firms in the same village,
but they have done no weaving for twenty years. Table and
household linens were the output of all of these firms, and
their market was found amongst wealthy families. There
are many old weavers living in the village, but there is no
attempt to utilize their skill and knowledge, and in another
few years it is probable that no trace will remain of the linen-
weaving industry of North Lopham.

The Sudbury, Haverhill, and Braintree silk factories
represent an outpost of the ancient Spitalfields weaving
industry. The ancestors of these, as of the Canterbury
weavers, came to England as Huguenot refugees. For
about one hundred and fifty years they carried on their trade
in Spitalfields, but in the early part of the last century, with
the increased use of machinery and the consequent incentive
to organization on a factory scale, a change difficult to
accomplish in the crowded district of the East End of London,
many of the chief firms moved out to Suffolk and Essex, and the
existing factories were established there. A number of the
home-workers on hand-looms remained in London, and many
of them, both men and women, are still to be found there,
weaving silk for the use of West End tailors. In Sudbury
and Haverhill, also, hundreds of weavers continue to work
in their own homes, as out-workers for the factories, in which
both hand- and power-looms are in use side by side. But, as
further improvements are made in the machinery, it becomes

possible to make more and more of the rich silks and velvets on the power-looms, and so the number of hand-weavers gradually decreases.

In Sudbury there is one factory in which only hand-weaving is done, but machinery is shortly to be introduced, although, as in the other factories, a few hand-looms will be retained for the weaving of such materials as the silk used for the lapels of dress coats, for the lining of the sleeves of men's coats, for umbrellas, and for ties and scarves. The making of umbrella silk is a speciality of Haverhill, where a London firm owns two small workshops, containing two and five hand-looms respectively, and employs also a couple of home-workers. There is, as well, a large factory in which only power-looms are used. Of the four hundred home-workers who used to weave velvet in Sudbury only two remain, working for London firms. There do not appear to be any out-workers employed on hand-looms in Braintree, but there are numbers of hand-loom weavers in the factories, as many as fifty being employed in one.

A single Spitalfields weaver has strayed into Surrey and works at Haslemere. He was originally an out-worker in the East End, and moved out to Essex, where he improved his position sufficiently to enable him later to set up in business independently. His reasons for migrating to Haslemere are not connected with the trade he plies. The materials which he makes are somewhat akin to those generally woven on the hand-looms in Essex and Suffolk, but he specializes in church hangings and fabrics for furnishing. At present he employs one boy, but hopes, if trade improves, to have two of his sons working with him.

Of the more recently established hand-weaving industries, that of the Lake District is the oldest and most important. The woollen-weaving industry was established in Westmorland by the Flemings in the fourteenth century, and until the latter part of the nineteenth century the locally produced wool was spun and woven in the farm-houses. Probably the isolated situation of the farms in this mountainous country, and the abundance of wool, added to the fact that the stormy weather of the long winter creates a need for indoor occupation, all help to account for the survival here of hand spinning and weaving when it had died out in other parts of the country. For the establishment of a new handicraft industry the Lake District was particularly suited both because of the existence here of traces of traditional craftwork and also because the beauty of the scenery makes it a favourite resort of artists and tourists, amongst whom is found a market for the goods. Thirty years ago a hand spinning and weaving industry was founded in Elterwater by a friend of Ruskin. This particular enterprise collapsed owing to the exposure of the fact that one of the weavers was selling factory-made materials as hand-woven, but two existing industries, one at Keswick and the other at Windermere, each claim to be the present representatives of the original organization. In the heyday of the Elter-water industry eighty spinners were employed and several men weavers. The aim of the promoters was to re-introduce the making of linen for their own household purposes by the farmers' wives. The first workers were men and women who inherited the skill of generations of home spinners and weavers, and in some cases the old looms were brought out from the cellars where they had been stowed away dismantled, and were set up again. Although the Westmorland weavers had long ago been famous for their woollens, it was the weaving of linen that was chiefly taken up by the new industries and linen is still the main product of the Lake weavers. There are a few working-class people amongst the present hand-loom weavers, and one or two farmers' wives carry on the craft as a spare-time occupation. A pattern-weaver from a factory has set up his own business here, and another man, formerly a silk-weaver at Braintree, combines weaving with an ordinary drapery business. But the idea of the founders of the industry, that country women might be encouraged to weave their own household linen, has proved to be impracticable. The cost of hand-woven linen is, in England, very high, since the thread must be bought from the big spinning firms, who are reluctant to sell small quantities. Raw flax can be bought, but it is expensive and to the spinning of it a great deal of time must be given. The weaving of linen also takes longer than that of woollen materials owing to the closeness of the work and the fineness of the threads, and only very skilled workers can spin and weave the finest linen required for household purposes.

There is a good deal of trade jealousy and rivalry amongst the hand-loom weaving industries of the Lake District. Great secrecy is preserved as to the identity of the out-workers employed on spinning, and the atmosphere generally is one of distrust. Accusations and rumours circulate freely, one worker alleging that others sell machine-made materials as their own work or foreign peasant work as locally made goods, and each inclining to consider that she only is upholding the principles of the true artist-craftsman. Amongst this group of craft-workers there seems to be none of the comradeship and co-operation which is often one of the benefits derived by the workers belonging to such a group, and which tends to encourage improvements in methods of work and economy of production. Probably the majority of the Lake weavers would scorn to consider questions of economy, deeming them unworthy of the notice of the artist, and so long as they continue to find in the tourist, with plenty of money to spend, a customer uncritical of prices, they will not be forced by competition to reduce their prices nearer to the ordinary market level.

There are weaving industries near Windermere, at Keswick, at Grasmere, and near Coniston. At one, which has been established for thirty-five years, wool and silk are woven as well as flax. Some wool is woven also by one other, but the majority of the weavers make only linen. In one case several men are employed at the looms and about twenty women out-workers on spinning, but most of the industries are on a much smaller scale, consisting of two or three workers each. A great deal of embroidery and ' Greek lace ' (drawn-thread work) is done on the linen by some of these firms, in fact, in some cases this is the main part of the work, and embroidery is also done on factory-made linen. Plain sewing and the making of children's dresses is combined with one weaving and embroidery industry, and another weaver sells a quantity of Italian embroideries.

The hand-weaving industries of the south-eastern counties are chiefly centred in Haslemere, Ditchling, and Canterbury. There are weavers in several other places, whilst an ex-service men's firm, of a type rather different from the others, is found at Horsham. In Sussex and the neighbouring counties, as in the Lake District, the weavers find a sale for their work amongst the many visitors, who are attracted there by the natural beauty of the county and its easy accessibility from London. There is a strong contrast between the Sussex group of weavers and that of the Lake District. There are pupils in many of the workshops of the former, who may, when they have mastered the craft, set up an independent weaving industry. The older weavers are not antagonistic to new enterprises, feeling that there is a real demand for hand-woven materials, and that the industry is capable of considerable development, which can best be brought about by a number of small firms, since they only can preserve the individual character of the work, by which hand-weaving is able to hold its own. The Sussex weavers were found to be far more willing to explain their methods and open their workrooms to visitors than were their fellow craftsmen in the Lake District, nor do they rely only on local customers but also show their goods at various exhibitions of handicraft work, where the prices can be compared with those of other weavers.

The oldest firm is one in Haslemere, which weaves cotton and linen. A woollen-weaving industry in the same place has three looms working and also employs about a dozen home spinners. The Ditchling weaver generally has three or four pupils working with her. At Canterbury there used to be forty girls spinning and weaving, but since the war no spinning has been done by this firm and only three or four girls were employed when it was visited in 1922. At Bognor a man and woman weave cotton materials and tweeds.

There are a number of hand-weaving industries in the south-western counties, among which may be mentioned the St. Ives Handicraft Guild, which includes weavers in cotton, and a weaving workroom at Clevedon, Somerset, where are woven tweeds and dress materials, notable for their individuality of design.

In Yorkshire there are, in the East Riding, two or three groups of weavers and one workshop with four looms. In the West Riding no trace remains of the once extensive hand-loom woollen-weaving industry. The ordinary commercial industry is now concentrated entirely in the factories, but two hand-loom weavers remain, one near Skipton and one at Clifford, who carry on the craft for a livelihood, in addition to other workers in the towns who weave only for a hobby.

Other hand-weaving industries are to be found in many places. In the Cotswold country there is a weaver at Broadway—a well-known centre for handicraft work—and two others at Sapperton, where it is hoped to work up an industry and employ girls to spin. Near Bromsgrove there is a weaving workroom in connexion with a furniture industry, and other workrooms, in which girls from neighbouring villages are employed, were found in Warwickshire at Hampton-in-Arden and in Lincolnshire at Coningsby.

At Newport, Essex, there is an interesting enterprise, in which five boys are being trained in weaving by a master-weaver, formerly a telephone operator. This weaver has also designed and built a small table-loom for weaving strips of material for trimmings, and he makes up furniture from old oak beams. Some very good work is done in this studio, and there is another weaving industry in the same town. There is a weaver at Thaxted, working in the room over the church porch. At Shottery, near Stratford-on-Avon, a group of three or four weavers carry on a successful industry, selling their goods in a shop in Stratford. In Cambridge several girls are employed, by a firm which has other activities, in weaving and repairing tapestry.

There are several industries organized for the employment of people who are mentally deficient or physically incapacitated for ordinary work. The Crippled Girls' Weaving School at Stratford-on-Avon was started fourteen years ago at Shottery as a private philanthropic enterprise by a lady who took crippled girls into her house and taught them to weave. It has gradually developed in scope and there is now a Home for the girls, and workrooms in which they learn and carry on spinning, dyeing, and weaving. It is under the management of a Committee and grants towards the maintenance of the girls are received from the Guardians, from whose Homes they come. The Home is also helped by a few private subscribers, for the majority of the girls are unable, owing to their physical disabilities, to work quickly enough to become self-supporting. Nevertheless, some excellent work is done and there is a good sale for it, but the scheme is under-capitalized.

At Cambridge, under the auspices of the Artificers' Guild, a number of persons who are slightly mentally deficient have been trained to weave materials of all kinds, from heavy tweeds for winter wear to the most gossamer-like silken fabrics. The industry, like that at Stratford-on-Avon, originated in a private scheme, in this case for training an epileptic boy to work on a hand-loom. It has taken the present organizer several years of patient work to produce the very beautiful fabrics which are now on sale in the shop of the Artificers' Guild. It is she who gives to the materials all their character of texture, colour, and design, the worker hardly realizing as he weaves what the finished article will be. The Stratford girls learn to exercise their own judgement to a greater extent, but they, although many of them are mentally undeveloped when they enter the Home, are intellectually superior to the Cambridge workers.

ii. *Raw Materials.*

Wool, flax, cotton, and silk are used by the hand-loom weavers, those in the Lakes weaving chiefly flax, whilst the majority of others make woollen materials, which are more quickly woven and can therefore be sold more cheaply, the wool also being easier to handle. There are a few weavers who specialize in making fine silk fabrics, which require more skill and delicacy of touch, and there are also the big silk industries in Essex and Suffolk. Several weavers use a certain amount of cotton, and mercerized cotton and flax are sometimes woven together to make 'uncrushable' linen.

Weavers in Yorkshire sometimes buy fleeces from the farmers of the Dales, whilst the Otterburn mills weave yarn from the Cheviot fleeces. Shetland wool is, however, generally the favourite. The wool, both white and black, of the cross-bred sheep which are usually kept in the West Riding of Yorkshire makes good, hard-wearing material, and the fleeces can easily be secured if ordered from the farmers before shearing-time. The black wool, used in its natural colour, which is not dead black but a dark rusty brown, is very effective in tweeds, especially when blended with other, dyed, wools. Shetland fleeces are particularly useful for natural greys and browns. Southdown wool is also very soft, and the Sussex weavers sometimes send Southdown fleeces to the Yorkshire mills to be spun. The weaver at Newport (Essex) uses wool from local sheep and carries out by hand all the processes necessary to its preparation, but more often the hand-weavers find that wool from local flocks is less suitable for their use than that which is to be obtained from a wool-stapler. The fleeces of the sheep kept in the south-western counties, for example, produce wool too coarse to be woven into the finer materials, although suitable for rugs and rough blankets, so neither the hand-weavers here, the Devonshire knitters, nor the local textile mills make any use of it.

The treatment of wool is a highly specialized industry, each process being carried on in a separate factory where the material is dealt with in bulk. Wool from the various parts of the same fleece will be found suitable for several different purposes. The fleeces are sorted and scoured, and may be combed, in the locality where they are produced, but are then sent to the great wool markets of Bradford and other Yorkshire towns, where the wool is bought by the cloth and

hosiery manufacturers, by whom it is dyed. Thus if the
hand-weavers buy fleeces from local farmers they must either
carry through for themselves all the processes of scouring
and carding the wool, in addition to the spinning, or else
send it to factories to be treated, this latter being an expensive
method because the big firms do not like the trouble involved
in dealing with small quantities which have to be kept separate.

Weavers may obtain raw wool, either from farmers or
from wool staplers, and have it spun in their own workrooms
or by outworkers, or they may buy yarn ready spun by
machinery. The latter is, of course, cheaper, and is largely
used to keep the price of hand-woven materials as low as
possible. In certain qualities, however, hand-spun wool
excels the machine-spun yarn and gives a special effect to
the material made from it, which cannot be obtained in any
other way. The yarn spun by hand is always slightly uneven,
and thereby causes a little irregularity in the texture of the
material which is liked by many buyers of hand-woven
stuffs, although an unskilled spinner may carry this uneven-
ness to excess, so that the cloth woven from her yarn will
be lumpy in places with thin, weak patches. But, particularly in tweeds and the coarser kinds of linen, the slight
irregularity which is characteristic of the nature of the flax
or wool is distinctly pleasing.

Materials woven by hand from machine-spun yarn are
apt to have a wiry texture, but certain skilled weavers have
shown, after careful experiment in the manipulation of this
thread, that beautifully soft and supple stuffs can be woven
from it. Yarn which is spun by hand is generally considered
to be stronger because less strain is put upon the fibres of
the wool or flax by the spinner, who can relax her pull when
necessary, than by the insensate machinery. Also, the
machine can spin the poorer sorts of wool, with shorter
fibres, whereas the hand-spinner can only deal with the long-
fibred material. Even a weaver who habitually uses mill-
spun yarn finds it useful to be able to spin any small quantity
of special wool which she may obtain and which is not
sufficient to send to a factory to be spun.

The supply of hand-spun yarn is inadequate to the needs
of the weavers and it is difficult to find women and girls who
are willing to take up spinning as a spare-time industry in
sufficient numbers to keep the weavers supplied. In addition
it seems to be impossible for any one who does not attain to
great dexterity and speed by giving her whole time to the
work, to earn a living wage by it. A Gloucestershire weaver

said, in 1923, that she could buy machine-spun yarn at from 3s. to 5s. a lb., whereas hand-spun wool from Scotland, bought through a middleman, cost from 17s. 6d. to 21s. a lb. ; she believed that she would be able to obtain it more cheaply by teaching local women to spin, but, to judge from the experience of others, this does not seem probable.

The majority of hand-loom linen-weavers use mill-spun flaxen yarn, although the Lake weavers issue a certain amount of raw flax to be spun by home-workers, and one or two other industries sometimes weave hand-spun flax. Raw flax of a suitable quality is difficult to obtain and very dear ; in fact, the mill-spun yarn, if bought in fairly large quantities, costs very little more than the raw flax. The best flax for fine linen comes from Courtrai, in Belgium, the waters of the River Lys in which it is steeped being said to possess certain properties which help to give it the soft and silken quality for which it is famed. Many hand-weavers buy mill-spun linen yarn from Ireland, and the now extinct linen industry at North Lopham (Norfolk) always used Irish flax for its linens. The price of raw flax rose from 1s. 6d. a lb., pre-war, to 5s. a lb., in 1923.

Cotton is only used by hand-weavers in the form of machine-spun thread, except when hand-spun yarn is obtained from India. One weaver suggested that beautiful mats and rugs could be made from coarse, hand-spun cotton, but in England the cost of labour for spinning it would be far too high in relation to the value of the material. The machine-spun cotton thread is generally obtained from the big Lancashire factories, although they often refuse to supply the small quantities required by the individual weaver. One woman who ordered 10 lb. of cotton from which to execute a special order was informed that the firm would not sell less than 50 lb., which would cost £6 and would be enough for 300 yards of material. For the weaver on a small scale, who relies chiefly on orders from private customers, this was a large outlay on material for which she might have no use for many months. A weaver who makes cotton dress lengths obtains cotton thread from the manufacturers of ' Duro ' fade-less fabrics. The French ' D.M.C.' cotton is used by another weaver for coloured borders on household articles, such as tray and table cloths. This can be bought in small quantities.

When silk is woven, machine-spun thread is generally used unless, as in the case of cotton, it is obtained from Assam or India ready spun by hand. The Indian hand-spun silk is rather coarse and, when woven, has the appearance of a very soft, loosely woven linen, but it drapes beautifully and does not crumple as linen does. The hand-spun silk from Assam costs about 15s. a lb. Some kinds of silk thread are easily obtainable in small quantities, and one firm will supply it in 1-lb. lots, dyed to any shade the weaver may require. From 1 lb. of silk six yards of material can be woven. A woman who weaves very delicate silken materials stated that she can obtain silk thread of the kind she requires only in 20-lb. lots, which involves a considerable outlay if several different shades are needed.

Weavers who possess several looms, including one of the heavy type suitable for the weaving of very coarse materials, often find that the making of various kinds of matting is a useful stand-by during any temporary failure of the demand for other woven goods. This kind of weaving is heavier work and of less artistic interest to the weaver, but moderately priced and durable mats of original colouring and design usually have a ready sale, especially when the weaver will make to order any size and shape required.

Amongst the materials which can be woven into mats are wool, jute, rags, and rushes. Jute is cheap and makes very durable matting. It must be bought from a firm of carpet manufacturers, as the wholesale dealers only sell it by the half ton. Coarse and rather rough woollen yarn is used for mats. The 'tapestry' rugs, alike on both sides, are woven on an upright tapestry loom. 'Turkey' rugs are made of wool knotted on to a wool warp, this not being a weaving process. Either of these two methods of mat-making is a slow one, and wool rugs are therefore expensive, the material also costing more than jute or rushes. Rags knotted together and woven into a string warp make firm but soft and easily cleaned mats, and by the blending of colours a good effect can be obtained. Rush-plaits are obtained from a firm of importers and the cost of carriage makes them a rather expensive material. English rush-cutters have failed to compete successfully with foreign firms in the production of rush-plait, although it is possible that a weaver in a district where the rushes grow could advanta-geously arrange to have them cut for her own use. Single rushes may be woven into a string warp to make rush-matting, and rush-plait may be woven in the same way. Other kinds of rush-matting are made by the rush workers by plaiting, not weaving, processes.[1]

[1] Vol. ii, *Osier Growing, Basketry Industries and Some Rural Factories*, Part I, Chapter III.

Rushes can be dyed, but the most pleasing colour-schemes are obtained by the selection and careful arrangement of rushes in their natural colourings, which range from dull green to a variety of brown and orange shades.

iii. *Processes.*

The raw material, be it silk, cotton, flax, or wool, must pass through a great number of processes before it can be woven into a fabric, or, in technical term, a web. Even after the weaving, some kinds of cloth must be scoured and pressed before they are ready for the market. It is possible for a weaver to obtain his yarn ready spun and dyed, so that the only processes which he must carry out himself are the setting up of the warp and the actual weaving. This is all that the Coventry ribbon-weavers do, because they are out-workers for a factory and their materials are prepared for them by machinery, the same being true of the silk and velvet weavers of Braintree, Haverhill, and Sudbury. But in the greater number of hand-loom weaving industries, which owe their foundation not only to their proprietor's necessity of earning a living but also to his or her interest as an artist and craftsman in the work, spinning and dyeing are also done, and in some cases, where wool is the material used, every detail of its preparation, from the carding of the raw fleece to the final weaving, is carried out in the one workroom. Relatively, however, a great deal more labour must be spent on the preliminary processes than on the actual weaving, and thus many hand-weavers find it impossible, through lack of capital or of other facilities, to do all these processes by hand, and some undoubtedly find it more profitable to weave by hand the yarn which has been prepared by the cheaper factory methods. But the individuality which is so important a characteristic of handmade goods can generally be best attained when the spinning and dyeing, as well as the weaving, are carried out under the direction of the master-craftsman.

It has already been pointed out that both flax and wool are sometimes spun by hand, but no instance was heard of in which the ' scutching ' of the flax was done by the handworkers, flax being obtained ready dressed from the mills. Wool, however, is sometimes bought from the farmer in the state in which it is shorn from the sheep, and it must then be carded and, sometimes, washed, before it can be spun. The carding or combing, although quite easy to do by hand,

takes a great deal of time, and adds considerably to the cost
of the woven material, whilst the ultimate effect is generally
considered to be no better. The wool is more often sent to
a mill to be treated, unless a very small quantity is being
dealt with. There is an opinion, however, that machine
carding arranges the wool in a long ribbon, or strand, of even
thickness, density, and length of fibre, and thus gives the
wool, although hand-spun, the even appearance of machine-
spun yarn. This certainly seems to be the result in the case
of the materials woven by Trowbridge workhouse girls, the
wool for which is carded in the Trowbridge mill but spun
by the girls themselves. By other workers, however, the
characteristic uneven appearance of hand-spun yarn is
obtained even when the wool is machine-carded, and it is
not clear whether the difference is due to any variation of
the method of carding carried on in the mill or to the way in
which it is spun.

The wool must, at some point in the process of manufacture, be cleaned of its grease. For scarves and other
loosely woven materials it may be washed before it is woven,
but tweeds of closer texture are best woven whilst the grease
is still in the wool and scoured afterwards.

Spinning may be done on a wheel or simply with a spindle,
but in England the former method is nearly always employed,
the latter requiring more skill on the part of the worker for
the production of a fine, even thread. Both flax and wool
are spun by hand for the Lake weavers and for several of
those in Sussex, and by the Trowbridge workhouse girls and
the crippled girls of Stratford-on-Avon. Some hand-weavers
in England obtain their hand-spun wool from the workers in
the ancient home-spun industries of Scotland, who become
expert spinners at an early age and therefore acquire the
necessary speed to enable them to work for piece rates which
are low compared to those asked by English village women,
who have learnt the craft late in life and probably give only
a few hours each week to the work. The Lake weavers are
still able to get a good deal of yarn spun by out-workers in
the villages, the industry having been revived in this district
before it had entirely died out, so that some of the workers
on traditional lines were still available, but even here it is
said to be increasingly difficult to get new workers to take
up spinning. Weavers in some other districts have tried
without success to persuade women in the neighbouring
villages to spin for them. A few workers would perhaps
take it up if higher wages could be paid than are generally

offered, but that would make the cost of the woven material
prohibitive. In a few cases spinners are employed in the
weaving workrooms, but since from eight to ten spinners
are needed to keep one weaver supplied this last arrangement
requires a great deal of workroom space if all the wool used
is to be spun by hand.

Spinning wheels can be obtained from Sweden, but a
worker who bought one in 1921 for £2 12s. said that it was of
poor material. There are a few English makers, notably one
in Somerset, whose price in 1922 was £4 4s., and a carpenter
who works for the Stratford-on-Avon weaving school,
through whom the wheels can be obtained at prices ranging
from £3 3s. to £5 5s. It was stated by a weaver in the south-
west of England, in 1922, that a wheel could be made for 30s.,
but few people seem able to obtain them so cheaply.

When sufficient yarn is ready the warp—that is to say,
the threads which form the groundwork of the stuff, running
from end to end of it—must be fixed on the loom before the
weaving, or threading of the weft threads through the warp
from side to side, can begin. The setting up of the warp
may take a day or even several days, the work being slower
and more laborious when finer threads are used. The warp
threads are first prepared on a warping mill, and the winding
of them on this device is an intricate process and has to be
done so that they will not entangle when placed on the loom.
They are wound first on a number of bobbins and then passed
round a big winder built of laths. The warp for the Coventry
ribbons, which is of silk, is sent to the weavers ready wound,
either on a big ball or else on immense wooden reels, but
generally weavers have to ' make ' the warp themselves.

The Coventry ribbon-weavers have a great deal of work
to do in winding the silk or cotton for the weft, first on to
' bobbins ' (reels) and then on to ' quills ' (which fit into the
shuttle), before it can be used for weaving, although this is
partly due to the fact that the material comes to them in the
form of very fine threads, several of which must be used
together in the weaving. For hand-weaving the winding of
the warp threads on to the bobbins to fill the shuttles is
usually a simpler process. Coventry weavers use a ' winding
engine ', but many of them do not possess this and so have
to pay another woman, known as the ' winder ', to do this
for them. The winding requires no particular skill and there
seems no reason why each weaver should not have a winding
engine of her own. The system is probably a relic of the days
when all the weavers had enough work to keep them busy

and one or more winders in each village would be constantly employed to supply them all.

One hand-weaver was met with who uses a loom fitted with an 'everlasting warp', which is wound, not on the hand-roll at the back of the loom, but on bobbins fixed to the wall behind the loom. A single bobbin has to be refilled from time to time as it is emptied, but the whole warp, once it has been set up, never has to be taken down and set up afresh. Thus the tiresome business of warping is avoided, but the weaver's choice of patterns is very limited, since she must always work on the same warp. The one weaver who uses this kind of loom makes nothing but cotton roller-towelling, and varies it only by occasionally working in a coloured stripe in the weft. A great deal of time is saved, and the material can therefore be produced more cheaply, which is a great advantage when it is made for a purely utilitarian purpose, but this system of an 'everlasting' warp would not suit any weaver the value of whose work depends on the artistry with which she blends the colours and the yarns for beauty of design and texture. Also, unless some very simple stuff is made, such as roller-towelling, for which there is sure to be a steady demand and which does not need to be varied in accordance with the changes of fashion, the weaver would not be able to find a market for any great quantity of goods of so similar a character. The one weaver who uses it had her loom built on the model of the power-looms in Manchester factories, which are used for the weaving of standard cotton materials.

In the simplest kind of weaving every alternate thread of the warp is lifted by one movement of the heddle. The intermediate threads are passed through intermediate eyelets suspended from a second heddle. The heddles are lifted in turn, by the working of the treadles below, the lifting of each one forming a 'shed' or space between the two sets of threads, across which the shuttle is thrown, thus passing the weft thread in and out of the warp, as in darning. In the small 'table-looms' used for weaving narrow pieces of trimming, the heddles are worked by hand-levers. In a complicated pattern there are a number of heddles, lifting various combinations of threads, and worked by a corresponding number of treadles. Some of the Coventry weavers use four-treadle looms for ribbons with patterned borders, in which case the warp threads for the border have to be wound on a separate hand-roll at the back of the loom. Some of these weavers remember using eight-treadle looms. But most modern hand-weavers use the simplest looms with only two treadles, and vary the plain woven pattern with coloured stripes, either in the warp threads, in which case the stripes run lengthways on the material, or in the weft threads, in which case the stripes run across the material and are made by using shuttles filled with different coloured threads. A more elaborate pattern, known as ' inlay ', can be made by threading the weft by hand in and out of the warp, over and under several threads, according to the pattern desired. This is a laborious method, but if only a few bands of the pattern are required, as, for instance, at either end of a long scarf, or for the hems of a dress-length, it is perhaps an easier one than the use of a four-treadle loom. The old weavers used very complicated looms, with as many as twelve treadles for the weaving of patterned materials, before the introduction of power-looms, but this kind of work is seldom, if ever, done on hand-looms nowadays. For the weaving of damask a special overhead attachment was used, and a loom of this kind is still worked by the Spitalfields weaver in Haslemere who weaves silk damask materials for furnishing purposes.

The width of material which can be woven on a hand-loom varies somewhat with the individual capacity of the worker. The distance across which she can comfortably throw the shuttle and also the space available for the loom must be considered when the loom is to be chosen. The ' web ' (the material on the loom which is already woven) is stretched taut on the loom, but shrinks together slightly when it is taken off ; a 56-inch loom makes material of any width up to 50 inches, a convenient measurement for curtains, and one woman weaver said that she could throw the shuttle this distance, but many find that 40 or even 36-inch wide material is as much as they can comfortably manage.

Before the power-loom was perfected and came into general use the device known as the ' fly-shuttle ' had been introduced on the hand-loom to hasten the process of weaving. When this method is used the shuttle is thrown across the shed by a mechanical device. The weaver only has to pull a string for each throw of the shuttle, and the work therefore requires less exertion and can be more quickly done. In the case of materials with coloured stripes in the weft this gain in speed is considerably reduced, because the shuttle must constantly be changed, and the weaver who throws the shuttle by hand can do this more easily. The fly-shuttle is used by a few hand-weavers, but more often by those who work most directly in competition with factory-made goods, as in the case, for example, of one who makes roller-towelling. Since they do not endow their goods with the value of individuality, they must avail themselves of this means of reducing the price.

In weaving with the fly-shuttle the left hand of the weaver works the batten, whilst the right hand pulls the cord to throw the shuttle, and both hands are thus held near together in front of the body, in a position similar to that of the ribbon-weavers, causing, it is said, a stooping position with the chest contracted. Advocates of the hand-thrown shuttle declare that it was the introduction of the fly-shuttle which led to the terrible prevalence of consumption amongst the old weavers, although their work in small and ill-ventilated cottages, and the long hours during which they had to sit at the looms in order to make a livelihood at the time when the competition of power-looms was leading to a reduction in their wages, must also have been contributing factors. Certainly the steady, rhythmical throwing of the shuttle by hand is pleasanter work than the more mechanical action of pulling the cord of the fly-shuttle, and experienced weavers who use the former method say that the time taken to throw the shuttle across a web of forty-inch wide cloth just allows the weaver time to change her feet on the treadles, so that the whole process provides exercise without any undue strain. One undoubted advantage of the fly-shuttle is that wider material can be woven by its use. A woman can easily weave anything up to two yards wide by this method, but, on the other hand, the fifty-inch materials which some weavers can make with the hand-thrown shuttle are as wide as would be needed for most purposes, whilst for dress materials forty inches width is generally sufficient. Weavers who throw the shuttle by hand say that by this means they can weave material of a finer texture, the more mechanical action of the fly-shuttle approximating to the power-loom and eliminating the artist's personal touch.

Some weavers have looms of both kinds; one woman, for example, has three flat looms, the largest, which makes material up to forty inches wide, being fitted with a fly-shuttle and a specially heavy batten. It is used for the weaving of tweeds, which are made of close texture and are therefore very durable. On the two smaller flat looms the shuttle is thrown by hand, and narrower materials, such as scarves and mats, are woven.

The table-loom, a variant of the flat loom, has already

been mentioned ; it is a small, light apparatus, easily moved about, and can be stood upon a table. These looms are built by a weaver at Newport, Essex; they are quite satisfactory for the weaving of bands of trimming, and even of narrow pieces of material of light weight. A lever serves instead of treadles to raise and lower the heddles.

The upright or tapestry-loom is another type, used for the making of tapestry mats or pieces of material for decorative purposes, coverings of furniture, hand-bags, or hat-bands. In this loom the threads are stretched vertically in a wooden frame or between two rollers, one high up and one exactly beneath it near the floor. The 'Axminster' carpets, made in Wilton and neighbouring villages, are woven on upright looms of a similar pattern. The 'chain' or ready-warped thread is sent from the big factory at Wilton to the smaller branch works and is put up on the looms by the girls who do the weaving. These warp threads of twine are stretched vertically from one roller to the other, so that the girls, three or four of whom work at each loom, seated on a bench, can conveniently put in the pieces of short wool that form the pile. After a row has been knotted on the warp a cross-thread is woven in to hold them in position. There are two methods of knotting ; one way is to take each cut piece of wool separately and to knot it in as in rug-work ; the other way is to knot in a long piece, making a row of loops which are cut afterwards to make the pile. The girls work with the pile side of the carpet towards them. The twine is harsh and roughens the hands, but the girls get used to it. The same weavers can do either plain or pattern work as required.

For tapestry weaving the pattern is sketched out on a card and fastened behind the warp threads, where it can be seen through them. The work is very slow, since the weft, instead of being thrown across from side to side in a shuttle, is threaded in and out of the warp by hand, yarn of several different colours being used and the design worked out in accordance with the sketch. The apparatus is very simple and in the Crippled Girls' Weaving School at Stratford-on-Avon, where small pieces of tapestry are woven, an ordinary table fork, used to beat down the weft as it is threaded in, is the only tool used in addition to the wooden frame in which the warp is stretched. Tapestry is generally woven on a warp of twine. Old pieces of tapestry are sometimes sent to these weavers to be repaired. A small tapestry loom is a useful and inexpensive addition to the outfit of a weaver who wishes

HAND LOOMS

The lower plate is reproduced by kind permission of Mrs. Mairet

to vary her output, but there is not a great deal of sale for the work because of its high cost.

None of the traditional loom-makers have survived in England, although it is probable that there are some in Ireland, where a recent effort has been made to revive and develop the old hand-loom weaving industry. There may also be some in Scotland, where the weaving of homespuns is still carried on in certain districts. Some of the hand-looms used for making the new patterns in textile factories are old ones which have been preserved. But the craft of making looms and spinning-wheels dies out before the actual spinning and weaving becomes extinct in any district, because both looms and wheels are strongly built and easily outlast the life of the spinner or weaver. As the number of workers diminishes, no new wheels or looms are required, any one taking up the craft for the first time being able to obtain old ones whose former owners are dead or have turned to other work. The Coventry ribbon-looms were almost certainly built by local craftsmen, but no traditional knowledge of their construction has survived, and when any part is broken the weavers find it difficult to replace. Most of the ribbon-looms present a ramshackle appearance, having been crudely repaired with pieces of string and leather. Probably not more than half a dozen new weavers have started work here within the last twenty years and so many of the younger women must, within that period, have given up weaving for more remunerative work in one of the local factories, that a loom would be easy to obtain. Many old ones must have been chopped up for firewood when the weavers died.

The old English looms were generally made of oak and are therefore very heavy. Modern weavers usually prefer looms of pine wood on the Swedish pattern, which is simpler than the English. Many of the Swedish looms and wheels have been imported to supply the weavers who have recently taken up the craft, and a few English carpenters have copied these models and can now build satisfactory looms. But, although the construction of a loom might appear to be fairly simple, it needs considerable skill and judgement, as one weaver found who had one made by a local carpenter copying a Swedish loom which she already had. The man did not understand the principles which should guide the loom-builder, with the result that his finished loom was badly balanced, with the weight in the wrong places, and was not easy to work. A carpenter at Stratford-on-Avon and another one at Clevedon, Somerset, have now become expert at building looms on the Swedish model, those made by the former being sold through the Crippled Girls' Weaving School, the promoters of which have helped him to perfect his work, and receive a small percentage of the profit on the looms.

Shuttles are even more difficult to make than looms. The construction of them varies considerably according to the work which is to be done. Those used by the ribbon-weavers are very small, made of boxwood, and should have metal noses, i. e. a narrow strip of steel let into the wood on each end, running up one side of the shuttle, over the tip and down the other side. These metal noses are liable to break off, and the workers cannot get them repaired or obtain new ones. If the metal is missing the tip of the shuttle is apt to become worn and roughened, so that it does not slide easily through the warp. The fly-shuttle is larger and heavier than the other, and is always fitted with metal tips and a wheel to make it run smoothly. Some hand-thrown shuttles also have this little wheel or roller on the bottom and the metal tips. There are tiny springs inside to hold the bobbin on which the thread is wound. The making of a shuttle requires fine and exact workmanship and there are few men in England who can do it satisfactorily.

A Haslemere weaver estimated the price in 1922 of a complete outfit for weaving as follows : Loom, £14 ; Warping-mill, £2 ; Reeds, of which one or two are needed, 12s. to 15s. ; Needles, 14s. a thousand ; Shuttles 3s. 6d., of which three or four are needed ; and Bobbin-winder, 15s. The price of 3s. 6d. for a shuttle seems a very low one in comparison with the cost as stated by other weavers. This would probably be the simplest type. A Yorkshire weaver said, in 1922, that she could not obtain a hand-thrown shuttle of the kind she needed for less than 15s., although she considered the actual value of it, with regard to the workmanship and material, to be only 4s. Her fly-shuttles cost 25s. 15s. for a hand-thrown shuttle was the price mentioned by another weaver in 1923. The Stratford looms could be bought at prices ranging from £5 10s. in 1923, although a few years ago as much as £15 was paid for an English loom. Imported Swedish looms were sold in 1921 for £12 each. In 1923 small tapestry looms could be bought at Stratford for £2 10s. each.

The weaving of velvet by hand, carried on at Sudbury by two out-workers, is a special process and a very slow one.

A grooved wire, $\frac{1}{24}$ inch thick, is thrust through the warp after every three throws of the shuttle. When there are three wires thus inserted the weaver runs a knife along the groove of the wire nearest to him, thus cutting through the warp threads which pass over it. The cut ends stand up and form the pile of the velvet. The finest dress velvet, such as that woven for Coronation robes, has 60 wires to each inch of the web, so the fineness of the silken threads of the weft can well be imagined. In furniture velvet there are 36 wires to the inch. The work is, of course, very slow and tedious.

When wool has been woven with the grease in it the cloth must be scoured and pressed before it is ready for wear. It is often sent to a textile mill for this process, a Yorkshire weaver, for example, sending her tweeds to Huddersfield, while the cloth woven in the Trowbridge workhouse is sent to the Trowbridge woollen mill. These large firms often dislike dealing with the small quantities which they receive from hand-weavers. This factory treatment also, is said to give the cloth an appearance approximating to that of machine-woven material and some weavers therefore avoid it.

The natural colour of flax is a pale brown, varying considerably according to the quality of the flax and to the method of its preparation. If white linen is required it must be bleached after weaving, and if this is done by hand it is a long and troublesome process, as the heavy rolls of linen have to be many times soaked in water and spread out on the grass in the sunshine, and the long strips of wet linen are difficult to move about. In the Lake District, where a great deal of linen is woven by hand, this is sold in its unbleached form, and when white linen is required by the weavers for the embroidery—work often carried on in connexion with the weaving industries here—it is obtained from the Irish mills.

The yarn is dyed before it is woven, and although many hand-weavers buy ready-dyed yarns, coloured by means of aniline dyes, others carry out the work of dyeing with vegetable dyes. Cotton is more difficult to dye than wool or silk, and flax is still more so. Hand-weavers who are interested in colour usually find great pleasure in dyeing their own yarns, and although certain shades cannot be obtained from vegetable dyes, yet this method, if used with skill and patience, can give very beautiful effects and great variety of colouring.

The great advantage of vegetable over aniline dyes is that the colours of the former are more durable, if the dyeing is properly done. But the processes are rather slow, and careful attention must be given throughout. It is said that there is need of further experiment and, what is more important still, of careful records of the experiments made, in order that the knowledge gained can be handed on to others. A very slight variation in the process may produce a considerable difference in the results. Since aniline dyes are a comparatively recent innovation, great stores of knowledge must have been amassed during centuries of experiment and practice in vegetable dyeing, but, through the break in the tradition, much of this seems to have been lost and modern weavers and dyers are working to rebuild the knowledge of this craft. It has been suggested that a laboratory in connexion with an Art or Technical School would serve a very useful purpose in this respect and, in fact, at the Leicester School of Art the question has been studied and information can be obtained.

Woollen yarn is the kind most often dyed by the hand weavers themselves. Flax is seldom treated owing to the difficulty involved and also owing to the fact that unbleached linen in the natural colours of the flax fibres is very beautiful, and is suitable for many purposes, whilst for a great variety the plain white (bleached) linen is preferred. Silk is fairly easily obtained from the manufacturers in small quantities dyed to the shade required, so it is not very often dyed by the weaver. Cotton can also be obtained ready dyed by patent processes in the so-called ' fadeless ' colourings and, although these are not always satisfactory, the very difficult process of dyeing cotton by hand with vegetable dyes would make this comparatively cheap material too expensive.

When dyeing is carried out in connexion with a weaving industry, a special stove for the dyeing vats and a large tank for rain-water are desirable. Some dyers make use of ready-prepared dye-stuffs in addition to the lichens, wood, and other vegetable products from which the dyes are obtained. Many of these grow in England, and some can be collected where they grow wild, while many others could be grown by the dyer. Crottles (lichens), giving brown and yellow colours, grow on the stone walls of the Yorkshire moors and elsewhere. Walnut husks are used for grey. Weld, a species of mignonette, also known as Dyer's Weed, which gives a yellow colour, grows on chalk or sandy soils and is found on the Sussex Downs. Spindle berries produce a very beautiful blue. Oak bark can be used for dyeing a rusty, brownish black and for lighter brown shades. Alder wood produces a reddish brown. Madder, used for red dyes, grows in the south of England and in France. Indigo, which is prepared from the stem of the indigo plant, is imported only in the form of a dye-stuff ready for use.

iv. *The Workers.*

As is pointed out by Miss Alice Clark,[1] ' from the general economic standpoint, the textile industries . . . in the history of women's economic development hold a position which is . . . unique . . . their labour was . . . indispensable to the textile industries, for in all ages and in all countries spinning has been a monopoly of women. This monopoly has been so nearly universal that we may suspect some physiological inability on the part of men to spin a fine even thread at the requisite speed, and spinning forms the greater part of the labour in the production of hand-made textile fabrics '. The making of linen, from the sowing and cultivation of the flax to the final processes of weaving and bleaching was often the work of women so long as this craft was practised chiefly as a home industry to provide for household needs. The weaving of woollen materials, however, was often considered to be work too heavy to be done satisfactorily by women and there were enactments against their employment on cloth looms. This continued to be mainly men's work until power-looms replaced the others. Where the ancient industry survives, the weavers, even of linen, are usually men, although there are still some women amongst the silk-weavers of Spitalfields, while the Coventry ribbon-weaving—the narrow web requiring less exertion—seems always to have been in the hands of women. Men weavers are to be found in the Lake District, in the survivals of the older industries in Somerset, in the silk and velvet factories of Braintree, Haverhill, and Sudbury, and as out-workers in these industries, and they were employed to weave the linens of North Lopham. But most of the newer industries have been started by women, and women are mainly employed in them, although the master weaver of one industry at Newport (Essex) is a man, who is training five boys, and the Spital-fields weaver who has settled in Surrey and worked up an independent industry there is also training a boy, whom he took on at the age of fourteen. A number of partially disabled ex-service men were trained in weaving, but very few of them seem to have been able to carry it on as an

[1] *The Working Life of Women in the Seventeenth Century.*

industry with any success. Their failure was probably due
to their inability to get into touch with suitable markets,
and also to the fact that few of them had enough artistic
ability or training to enable them to give their products the
individual stamp in which much of the value of hand-made
materials consists. Too often the cloth made was in stereotyped patterns, and the use of mill-spun yarn and the final
scouring and pressing by machinery gave it the appearance
of a factory product. Although attempts are made to
speed up production by the use of the fly-shuttle, the hand-
weaving industry is bound to fail if it comes into direct
competition with factory production. The hand-made
material may have greater durability than that which comes
from the factory, but few people will pay a higher price
for hand-work unless it *looks* different. One or two may buy
from sympathetic motives, but an industry depending on
the charity of its customers will not thrive for long.

As regards the employment of men in the hand-weaving
industries in general, some people still maintain that women
cannot weave so well. In one of the largest of the Lake
industries only men are employed on the looms, and the
woman who organizes it stated that women could not throw
the shuttle across the broader webs and that their weaving
has not a tight enough texture owing to their lack of strength
in beating up the slay, which is the most strenuous work in
weaving heavy woollen materials. Certainly the looseness
of a great deal of hand-woven tweed is a serious drawback,
since it causes it to pull out of shape when worn. Judging
from the very best work of women weavers, it may be con-
cluded that they are capable of weaving, with the hand-
thrown shuttle, materials of good close texture in silk, cotton,
flax, and wool, of any width up to 36 or 40 inches, although
they do not excel in the weaving of the very heaviest kinds
of tweed and cloth. Probably the faults which are sometimes to be found in their work are more the results of insufficient training or of carelessness, than of actual incapacity.

The reason that a greater number of women than of men
is to be found in the industry at the present day, is one which
applies to all the home crafts and industries, namely, that
women more often enjoy that independence, untrammelled
by the necessity of supporting a family, which enables them
to launch out on a somewhat risky enterprise. When the
industry has developed to such an extent that they begin
to need an assistant, they often find it convenient to take
as pupils one or two other women who are learning the craft

WEAVERS AT WORK

with a view to setting up a new independent industry or to
practising it as a hobby. If regular employees are required,
the weaver in a rural district can sometimes find village
girls who will not require very high wages, for few of the
hand-weaving industries are so commercially successful that
they can afford to pay what would be a suitable wage for
a fully skilled man. But there are a comparatively small
number of employees of any kind in the industry, although
a group of two or three weavers often work together co-operatively with success. The number of employees engaged in
spinning is far larger, partly because the bulk of the labour
which goes to making any piece of material entirely by hand
is devoted to spinning, and also because spinning can be
done as a spare time home industry by women otherwise
engaged on household duties. Many weavers who have
chosen this craft because of the opportunities which it offers
for the exercise of their talent for artistic creation, prefer
to work alone, or with only one helper, because they consider
that the originality of design can only be expressed in their
own handiwork.

In many districts the weavers seem to have no difficulty
in finding local girls or women to work as apprentices or
employees. The Broadway worker has two apprentices
from the village, four women are employed on the looms in
a workroom near Bromsgrove, and ten spinners, old women
who have recently been taught, work here in their own homes
on wheels which are lent to them. Out-workers are employed
on spinning in a good many cases, particularly in the Lake
District, where at one time there were as many as eighty
women working in their homes for one firm, although the
number has since been reduced to twenty. Some of the
Sussex weavers employ a number of home spinners, both
village women of the neighbourhood and also a few well-to-do
women in different parts of the country who do it as a hobby.

On the outskirts of a little town in Yorkshire several looms
have been set up in a workroom and a number of girls, most
of them shop assistants in the town, spend their spare time
in weaving under the direction of the promoter of the scheme
—which was designed to provide the girls with a part-time
occupation in creative work. The girls receive wages, but
not, apparently, at rates high enough to provide them with
a livelihood even if they were to work at weaving as a full-
time employment. It is said that the industry yields no
profits, although there seems to be a good sale for the products. The girls become fairly proficient after about a year,

during which period a few hours weekly are spent at the loom.

In one of the Haslemere industries girls are taken on as apprentices at the age of fourteen, on leaving the elementary school ; it was stated here that there is considerable competition amongst the girls whenever any vacancy occurs and that the industry is seldom able to admit all who apply. There are usually from four to six apprentices working in these weaving rooms, although in 1921 when a visit was paid, trade was very slack and there were only four.

In this and in other cases the village girls and women were said to take the keenest interest in the craft and particularly to enjoy working out new patterns. From many weavers, however, the complaint is heard that they cannot get village girls or women to take any interest in the crafts of spinning and weaving. One Yorkshire weaver, for example, who finds it difficult to execute unaided the large orders which she often receives, has tried without success to find another woman who would work in partnership with her or as an assistant. Other weavers speak of the same difficulty, one Lincolnshire woman expressing the opinion that tradesmen's daughters are more willing to take up the work than are the girls in farm workers' families. The same story is told with regard to spinning. One or two weavers who had offered to teach local girls and women to spin, and to find employment for them, had met with no enthusiasm, although there is said to be a considerable demand among weavers for hand-spun wool. In many cases it is evident that the rate of payment for spinning is not sufficiently attractive, particularly in cases where local factories offer alternative employment.

Thus, several cases indicate that the crafts of spinning and weaving are readily taken up by village women, who find in them a source of interest and a sufficiently profitable whole or part-time occupation ; whilst other cases—greater in number—indicate the very opposite, namely, that village women do not find this industry attractive and that, even in villages where there is no competition from other forms of employment, there is no one willing to take up the work. What is the explanation of these contradictions ? There seem to be four chief factors in the problem.

The first is locality : in districts, such as the Lakes and Sussex, where there are groups of handicraft workers, many of whom have been settled there for years, a general interest in handicraft work has been aroused, and small industries have grown up and prospered under the eyes of the village

THE WORKERS 35

people. But in other districts, where the idea of any such
enterprise is a new one, the conservative villager, who tends
to distrust anything strange, probably considers it something in the nature of a fad or freak, which can hardly be
connected with a steady source of income, and in which it
would be better not to be involved. It is also probable that
in these centres of handicraft work where there are opportunities for the sale of a good deal of the produce to visitors,
without the expense of sending it to shops and exhibitions,
somewhat higher wages can be paid, but the information
on this point is scanty. Another point in connexion with
the importance of the locality of an industry, already
suggested in Chapter II, page 11, is that it is easier to revive
the spinning and weaving industries in a district where they
have only recently died out, and where the old skilled workers
are still to be found, than to establish them in a place where
all traces of the craft have long ago been lost. In at least
one of the cases mentioned above, where there was difficulty
in obtaining workers, it was due to the competition of local
factories in the labour market, but in the case of the industry
near Bromsgrove, where factory rates of wages are paid to
the weavers, this difficulty has been overcome, although it
is not clear whether the industry can really bear the expense
of such high rates of pay. Most of the hand-weaving work-
rooms are situated in rural districts where there is hardly
any other opening for employment, except on the land or in
domestic service.

The second factor is that of the expense of the necessary
apparatus for weaving or spinning. Weavers are usually
employed in the workrooms on looms belonging to the
employers, but employers who would undertake to provide
home spinners with work and to teach them free of charge,
often expect the women to provide their own wheels, and
the price of about four guineas for one of these would be
enough to discourage a cottage woman. Wheels are loaned
to the spinners near Bromsgrove, and in this case ten women
in the neighbourhood have taken up the work. But in many
of the small, newly started industries capital is not available
for the purchase of a number of wheels. The primitive
method of spinning with only a distaff and spindle does not
seem to have been tried in England, probably because more
skill is needed to produce a fine thread by this means.

The third factor is the rate of wages. Since there are so
few employees of any sort in the industry, and many of these
are in the position of apprentices, it is difficult to draw any

D 2

general conclusions as to current rates, but in many cases the wages offered have been very low, and it is usually considered that it is impossible to earn a livelihood by spinning.

The fourth factor may be summed up as the personality of the weaver. The promoters of these industries are often strangers to the district and sometimes suffer from a lack of understanding of rural conditions and of the way in which to win the sympathy of the village woman. Some of them, whilst putting a very high value on their own work, are unwilling to pay the weaver as a skilled worker, even if they can afford to do so. If the apprentices were to receive more training in designing, and were encouraged to work out patterns and colour combinations of their own, they might take more interest in the work, and probably many of them would develop real talent in this direction. The plan carried out in one of the Haslemere industries, of allowing the apprentices to return to the workroom after working hours and weave materials for their own use at the cost to themselves only of the yarn used, gives them not only an opportunity for additional practice but also the satisfaction of being able to create something for their own personal possession, and so stimulates their interest in the craft. Concerning this factor of personality it is hardly safe to generalize, but the failure of certain industries would seem to be at least in part due to it.

Information concerning the wages paid for spinning wool is incomplete, but it was stated in the Lake District that 4s. a pound was paid before the war for the spinning, and that most of the part-time workers brought in only a pound each week. One estimate is that a woman can spin an ounce in an hour. Another informant declared that it is possible for a good worker to spin one pound of wool in a nine-hour day. Another estimate from the Lake District was that a full-time spinner earned 18s. a week before the war, and from 25s. to 30s. a week in 1921. In Sussex the rate paid for spinning in 1921 was 6d. an ounce, which, at the speed of one ounce an hour, would represent a weekly wage of about 18s. for full-time work. In 1922 one weaver stated that the cost of spinning one pound of Shetland wool was 15s. in Scotland, but the labour involved in this is more than that of spinning ordinary yarn for tweed weaving.

Since there are so few employees in the hand-weaving industry and the conditions of employment vary considerably in different instances, it is impossible to make any general statement as to the usual rates of wages. Instances of the rates said to be current in certain districts can, however, be given. Mention has already been made of the industry near Bromsgrove where the rates paid are equivalent to those of the factories in the neighbouring town of Redditch. It was stated in 1921 that the man employed in a textile mill as pattern-weaver on a hand-loom, who is often an over-looker also, could earn £5 to £6 a week, but he would be a particularly skilled weaver. At this time the Westmorland weaver who gave this information said that he hoped to employ three or four men if the market, which was affected by the trade depression, should improve, and that they would receive about £3 or £4 a week in wages. He himself had ceased to work for one of the weaving industries of the district through a disagreement as to the rate at which he should be paid, so probably the £3 to £4 which he considers a suitable wage is a higher one than that usually paid.

In the Haslemere cotton weaving industry apprentices are taken on at the age of fourteen and work without wages for two weeks, after which they receive a small remuneration, which is gradually increased. After one year's training they become really useful, and at the end of two years they have become proficient and can earn 30s. in a 39-hour week. The boy apprentices in a Newport (Essex) industry were earning 12s. a week in 1922 whilst still very inexperienced. One weaver stated that adults who come to her as pupils master the craft in from three to six months.

There is more definite information as to the wages earned by weavers who are in the position of outworkers for factories. They are always paid by piece-rates per yard of material woven, but in reckoning the amount which they can earn, not only the time taken in the actual weaving of the material must be considered, but also the time taken to set up the warp. It is to the advantage of the weaver to set up a warp for as many yards as possible at one time, as he is not paid separately for this work. In this respect the Coventry ribbon-weavers are at a disadvantage, for only such ribbons as are needed in small quantities are given to the out-workers to be woven by hand, and the weaver considers herself lucky if she ' gets in ' for 36 yards or more in a week, instead of only 18 yards, as may be the case. She is still more fortunate if in two consecutive weeks she ' gets in ' for ribbons requiring the same warp, which thus does not have to be set up again. In addition to the making of the warp, she also has to wind the bobbins and quills before she can begin the weaving. One of the ribbon-weavers stated that the preliminary work took from two to three hours, but this seems a low estimate if the winding, as well as the making of the warp, be included. The amount earned by them is very small. One worker estimated that the maximum possible earnings in a week would be £1, but she would have to work very long hours for that, much longer than factory hours. As a matter of fact, the ribbon-weavers never get enough work now to enable them to earn as much as £1. They stated that a good worker could make in an hour three yards of ribbon about 1½ inches wide with cotton weft, and that, of another similar ribbon, 2 inches wide, with 30 throws to the inch (i. e. 30 threads of the weft), it would be hard work to make two yards in an hour, the pay being 1½d. a yard. Although the work on a four-treadle loom is rather more skilled, it is no better paid, but, if anything, rather worse, for it takes longer to do and the extra price paid per yard hardly makes up for this. Out of the meagre pittance which the women earn most of them have to pay a few pence to the winder. The ends of warp left over, when the weaver has finished the required length of ribbon and cut it off, are known as ' thrums ' and are the perquisite of the weaver.

The men who weave silk and velvet for the Essex and Sudbury factories are somewhat better paid than the ribbon-weavers, although, especially in the case of velvet-weaving, the rates are decidedly low. A weaver stated that he could make a yard of furniture velvet a day and that he received 5s. 6d. for this work. Of dress velvet he could make only half a yard a day. It takes him a week to set up the loom, but he is able to make the warp for a length of about fifty yards, which would represent at least eight weeks' work on weaving. When the extreme fineness of the threads which are used and the intricate process of weaving and cutting the pile [1] are considered, this very slow rate of production can be understood. Working six full days in the week he would make six yards of furniture velvet, for which he would be paid 33s., but for every eight weeks of weaving one week of setting up, for which he is not paid, must be reckoned, so that the average flat rate over nine weeks would be about 29s. a week at the maximum. He himself said that he reckoned the rate as about the equivalent of 27s. weekly.

A schedule of the rates paid for the weaving of umbrella silk at Haverhill showed at January 1st, 1920, an increase of 100 per cent. over those of March 5th, 1898. In 1923 the

[1] See p. 29.

earnings were said to be about £2 a week, and often less because of the scarcity of work. The maximum possible earnings in a week were given as £2 5s.

Weaving and spinning are crafts which have for some time been utilized for the employment of the blind, the crippled, and those who suffer from slight mental deficiency. At the Barclay Workshops for Blind Women in London and Brighton there is ample evidence of the excellent work which blind people can do on the loom, under efficient direction. In the rural districts investigated, there were several examples of weaving industries in which the workers are feeble-minded or physically disabled to some extent, and in some cases the work done by these people is of the highest quality. The Government schemes for training partially disabled ex-service men in weaving, and the frequent failure of those trained to establish an industry on a firm basis, have already been mentioned.

In the case of the weaving carried on by feeble-minded girls in a Trowbridge institution, there was no idea of making these girls independent, but the occupation is good for them and brings them happiness and also a little money to spend as their own. It may afford, as it develops, some substantial contribution to the expense of caring for the feeble-minded, which is a necessary but costly charge on the rate-payer. These girls seem to learn both weaving and spinning without difficulty, although they are slow at the work and a variety of occupation is needed because of their lack of ability to concentrate on anything for long at a time. The same applies to the crippled girls employed on spinning and weaving at Stratford-on-Avon, who are, in the majority of cases, mentally stunted as well as physically unfit. When they first enter the school from the Guardians' Homes they have received little education and have developed no sense of responsibility ; thus they are very difficult to train. After they have worked in the school for some time wonderful improvement is shown in the development both of character and of intelligence, and two of the girls have become sufficiently skilled and dependable to leave the Home, live by themselves, and earn their own living. One is employed in the school as a tapestry weaver and the other as dyer and assistant teacher-draughtswoman, and they earn from 10d. to 10½d. an hour. But the majority of the girls, owing to their physical disabilities, can never attain to the speed and skill of able-bodied workers and will never become self-supporting. One of the difficulties of organizing this kind of industry is that there is no outlet for those trained, since the ordinary weaving industries cannot afford to take such slow workers and pay them enough to support themselves. Thus the school can only take for training a limited number of girls for whose output it is able to find a market. Most of the girls can work for a seven-hour day if the work is varied, but some do less. Those who are too lame to work the treadles of a loom can weave tapestry, as for this they sit at the upright frame and do all the work with their hands.

At Cambridge an epileptic boy and several others, either mentally or physically incapacitated from earning their living otherwise, are employed in a weaving studio under the auspices of the Artificers' Guild. These weavers are paid by piece-rates and are able to support themselves. Their capacity is varied, some being able only to make the coarser materials, while others acquire the technique of the craft to perfection, and produce the most delicate silken fabrics.

The question which arises, when the employment of these feeble-minded and physically incapacitated people in weaving industries is considered in relation to other industries of the same kind in which normal people are employed, is whether the former, subsidized as they must be because the workers cannot attain sufficient speed to compete on equal terms, may not undersell the latter and tend to cause a reduction in the wages of normal weavers. In the Trowbridge institution no attempt is made to render the industry self-supporting, and the cloth is sold at prices which are far below those of other hand-woven materials, and almost certainly less than the cost of production of such materials could possibly be. These 'Semington Homespuns', as they are called, were sold at a London exhibition in 1922 at prices from 5s. a yard, other excellent specimens, 31 inches wide, being priced at 6s. and 6s. 6d. a yard. This is only the price of factory-made cloth, and, indeed, these homespuns were at first sold only through the Trowbridge mill, the owner of which agreed to take all that the girls made. In this way the industry did not really compete with hand-weaving, but when the materials are sold at handicraft exhibitions they are in direct competition with the products of other hand-loom industries. This problem indicates the need for some agreement amongst hand-weavers as to a standard scale of prices and wages. If the work of the unfit were priced at a rate which would cover the cost of production by normal workers adequately paid and provide a reasonable profit, then the subsidy which these industries for the subnormal receive should serve to compensate for the slowness of these workers. The output of the Stratford-on-Avon and of the Cambridge weavers is sold at prices approximating to those charged in any other hand-weaving industry. The Stratford industry has not been self-supporting, up to the present, owing to under-capitalization, but it is hoped that the financial position may be improved and that, in the future, with the help of the Guardians' grants towards the maintenance of the girls, it may be able to pay its way. The Cambridge industry enjoys special advantages in that it is run as an adjunct to the Artificers' Guild, which has a shop in Cambridge for the sale of jewellery, pottery, metalware, and other work of various individual craftsmen, so that there are excellent opportunities for the sale of the woven goods also. Prices here are high, but they are justified by the excellence of the workmanship and by the beauty of design, which is due to the organizer of the industry. In this case the work of weavers who are mentally subnormal can be sold side by side with the work of other craftsmen at corresponding prices and without any special appeal to the charity of the buyers. This weaving industry would not be able to stand by itself, but, combined with the sale of other handicraft work, it is beginning to show some profits, although the market is subject to fluctuations and the organizer had to keep the work going without any profit to herself for two years whilst she was ' feeling ' for a market.

v. Business Organization.

Various types of organization are to be found in the weaving industry, ranging from the part-time individual worker who aims at making some addition to an income derived from other sources, and who often makes little or no attempt to organize her business on systematic lines, to the workrooms under the direction of an individual or of some guild for the production and sale of handicraft work. There are also a number of small industries in which the only workers are the two or three weavers who are partners in the business. As a weaving industry develops, the branches of hand-spinning and dyeing are generally included, and this necessitates the employment of additional workers. Few weavers are so fortunate in the locality of their industry that they are able to sell all their output from the workroom itself or a neighbouring shop. It is therefore of great advantage to them to be connected with one of the organizations for the sale of handicraft work, such as the Peasant

Arts Guild, to which is affiliated one of the Haslemere industries, or the Artificers' Guild, under whose auspices the Cambridge weaving studio is run, or the Home Arts and Industries Association, whose membership includes many hand-weavers and spinners throughout the country. Such organizations also afford to scattered individual weavers the opportunity to meet together and discuss questions which affect them all, particularly questions relating to rates of wages and the prices at which their goods are to be sold. At present there seems to be a lack of co-ordination amongst them and great variations are found in the prices asked for very similar goods. The few who turn out poor work, probably through having set up as independent workers before they were sufficiently experienced in all branches of the craft, and others who put a fantastic price on their goods out of proportion to the value of the work and material, all tend to bring the industry into disrepute or to cause its products to be regarded as only an expensive luxury for the wealthy. Many weavers cater for simpler tastes and shallower pockets and show that the worker on the hand-loom can very well combine in her output great beauty of texture and colouring with good wearing qualities. The value of the small workshop, in which the individual taste and judgement of each worker is given full scope, is of great importance in this industry, but, on the other hand, the weavers might, by co-operation, solve some of the problems connected with the obtaining of raw materials, the spinning of wool by hand, and, in some cases, the finding of a market for their goods. The industry, in its revived form, is a comparatively new one, and its future is likely to be affected considerably by the way in which these problems are solved.

vi. *Markets.*

To the handicraft worker on a small scale a connexion with a suitable market is of the greatest importance but is often difficult to obtain. Inability to sell her goods may be due to the fact that she has not gauged the public taste correctly or expressed in her work qualities sufficiently attractive and arresting to gain customers, but, on the other hand, it may be, and often is, due to the fact that she has not found a means of displaying her wares to those people who would be likely to buy them.

Hand-woven goods cannot as a rule be disposed of through the ordinary commercial channels for the sale of textiles.

They appeal to a somewhat limited class, although some weavers say that the market seems to be extending and that public taste is inclining towards a greater appreciation of handicraft work. The buyers of the products of the hand-loom are people who appreciate beauty, particularly beauty of texture, in materials for their own wear and for the furnishing of their houses. For furnishing purposes, particularly where curtains and coverings for chairs are required to match some decorative scheme, hand-woven fabrics are often needed, and one or two hand-weavers specialize in materials for furnishing. It is said that 1,000 yards of any one pattern is the least that is ordinarily made on a power-loom, whereas the hand-loom weaver can make a few yards of any pattern at a cost which is not very much greater.

In connexion with the marketing of their goods the first need of the weavers is a link between the isolated worker and the public. Materials cannot satisfactorily be sold unless the customer can see beforehand what he is buying. Neither descriptions nor illustrations can convey exactly the nature of the goods, but, if pieces are to be cut off for patterns, a large proportion of the short lengths of material which are made will quickly be used up. In the case of ' dress lengths ' with bands of woven pattern planned to come at the hems or wherever decoration may be desired, no patterns can give an exact idea of the whole piece of woven stuff. It is thus essential that the weaver should have an opportunity of displaying her goods in an adequate space before likely customers. The exhibitions of handicraft work help to provide this opportunity, but only on a few occasions during the year, and this is hardly enough for any one except a part-time worker. There is also to be considered the expense of conveying the goods to London or another centre, and of hiring a stall, the necessity for the worker's presence, and her expenses for travelling and lodging. All this must be covered by the sales effected during the short period of the exhibition. Many weavers find that the value of a stall at an exhibition repays all this expenditure of money, time, and trouble, but nevertheless, this seems an expensive and cumbersome method of selling goods. Ordinary shops will seldom deal with the output of hand-weavers, because, like that of other handicraft workers, it is too small in bulk, not sufficiently standardized, and cannot be produced to order quickly enough, to suit their purposes. Moreover, since the amount of labour necessary to the production of hand-woven goods—especially if they are also hand-spun—is so great, the prices must be kept as low as possible if a ready sale is hoped for, and if several middlemen were to reap a profit the retail price would be too high for many customers.

Another difficulty is, that good craftsmen are often lacking in business experience or capacity, and it is as craftsmen rather than as business men that the majority of hand-weavers have set their enterprises on foot. There is also the need to 'feel for a market' and to adapt the things made to its demands. This may be a slow and costly process, especially with the more expensive kinds of material, for which the market is necessarily limited.

A minor difficulty is that tailors are reluctant to make up any materials other than those which they themselves supply, and, if they consent to do so, include in their charge to the customer the amount of the commission which the tailor would otherwise receive from the manufacturer for the sale of his goods. Weavers of tweeds would be considerably benefited if they could form business connexions with tailoring firms which would supply and make up their materials.

The importance to weavers of their connexion with an assured market is shown by the instance of the Winterslow industry, which was revived amongst small-holders by a lady who for some years made herself responsible for the selling organization. Subsequently she handed over the business, and from this time it declined, the men being unable to keep in touch with the former customers or to find new ones.

Several different methods of marketing their goods are commonly made use of by hand-weavers. One is by sale through a shop in the neighbourhood of the weaving-room or from the workshop itself. This system is employed to the best advantage in cases where various kinds of handwork—metal work, jewellery, furniture, pottery, toys—produced by local craftsmen, are sold. There are shops of this kind in Cambridge, Broadway, and elsewhere. Here the hand-woven materials may be displayed to good advantage in company with other things of artistic value. Some of the Women's Institute shops in different parts of the country sell the output of local weavers, charging only a small commission on sales. In some cases, however, sale through a shop may prove expensive if the district is not a suitable one, or if there is not sufficient variety of stock. A hand-weaving industry in the south-west of England, which employed two workers and ran its own shop for the sale of the materials, found it necessary to charge for them double the actual cost of making and material in order to cover all overhead expenses and make some profit.

In any district where there are a number of wealthy visitors the local shop or the workroom which is open to customers may provide a good market. This is seen in Sussex, at Broadway, and at Stratford-on-Avon, and especially in the last place, for Americans seem to be particularly susceptible to the charm of novelty. (The Lake District is also a very good centre.)

A few weavers are in touch with handicraft shops at some distance from them to which they send their work. For example, the furnishing materials woven at Kirkby Moorside are largely made to the orders of architects with whom the organizer of the industry is in touch, but some are sold through furnishing firms. The Spitalfields weaver at Haslemere, who does the same kind of work, has an agent in London through whom he obtains orders. This weaver and some others sometimes receive special orders for church hangings.

A few of the smaller industries dispose of a large part of their output to friends of the weaver, but this sort of market is not likely to absorb even the output of a single worker for very long, although it may be helpful during the early days of an industry.

It is difficult to give any representative examples of the prices of hand-woven materials or to compare these with the cost of similar stuffs made by machinery. In both cases the novelty or originality of a design may endow a piece of material with a temporarily exaggerated value. Amongst the products of hand-weavers there is so little attempt at any standardization of price, and the market value of the material depends so much not only upon the artistic talent and the craftsmanship of the individual weaver, but also upon her method of marketing, her reputation, and her own estimate of the value of her work, that it is difficult to find an average.

vii. *Prospects.*

On the whole, the demand for hand-woven materials seems to be on the increase, a number of new industries having been started since the war, and there seem to be few actual failures, except perhaps among the ex-service men, many of whom had neither the business capacity nor the knowledge of markets necessary for the success of such an enterprise. Artist craftsmen who can produce good original designs and colour schemes and carry them out—spinning, dyeing, and weaving, with finished technique—find no difficulty in disposing of their wares.

One of the points of greatest importance in the future development of the industry is that of training in technique, design, and business methods. One or other of these three points, which are of almost equal importance for the founder of an industry, is too often neglected. One of the weaving schools stated that a course of from three to six months was generally sufficient, but, although weavers would probably acquire technical facility in that time, they would not be fitted to carry on an independent business.

Another problem on the solution of which the future of the industry greatly depends, is that connected with the hand-spinning of yarn. On the one hand there is the cost of employing the number of full-time workers who would be required to supply even one hand-weaver ; on the other, there is the difficulty of the irregularity of the supply, both in quantity and in quality, of the supply from part-time home-workers. Spinning has met with no success as a cottage industry in the south-western counties and is not likely to succeed there. In the Lake District the weavers still seem able to obtain a considerable supply of hand-spun yarn from local village women, but even here it was said that it becomes increasingly difficult to find spinners. The whole problem is mainly one of wages, and the cost of having the work done by hand. It is possible that spinners who could spend more time on the work than those now employed generally do, could acquire sufficient speed to make the occupation a remunerative one. If wheels could be bought at a lower price, or the simple distaff and spindle could be used, the problem would be somewhat simplified. Spinning is in some respects an ideal craft for a home industry. It is easily learnt, does not require very close concentration, is not particularly tiring or trying to the eyes, can be well done in a poor light, and the wheel does not take up a great deal of space. But unless spinners can increase their working speed, by spending more time at the wheel, the industry will not be able to bear the cost of hand-spun yarn.

Other problems, connected with the high cost and, sometimes, the impossibility of obtaining raw materials in sufficiently small quantities, and with the isolated worker's inability to get into touch with suitable markets at a reasonable expense, have already been referred to.

For purely utilitarian purposes hand-weaving is almost entirely superseded by the power-loom. This is illustrated by the instance of hop-pockets, the large sacks for hops, which were woven by hand in Kent until about ten years ago. In a factory one man can make 500 hop-pockets in a day, whereas one woman could in a day weave only 50 on a hand-loom. In such a case the slight superiority of the hand-made article could not compensate for the far greater economy of machine-production. The weaving of roller-towelling on hand-looms by one or two weavers has already been referred to ; these workers are able to sell this cotton material at the ordinary shop prices, but they could not afford to sell it at wholesale prices, and difficulties of distribution would prevent them from finding a market for any large quantity, nor could enough profit be made on it to enable them to employ labour for the weaving. This material is therefore unlikely to be made except by a few individual workers at times when their production of other goods exceeds the immediate demand.

An interesting point in connexion with the ancient weaving industries is that although in some cases the modern industries have been developed from the relics of older ones in the district, yet it is noticeable that often there is no point of contact between the modern ' arts and crafts ' movement and the older industries in the same neighbourhood. For example, the existence of the Coventry ribbon-weavers is unknown to most people in Warwickshire, excepting their neighbours in the villages in which they work and the people directly connected with the industry. There are a number of modern hand-weavers in the county, and it is possible that if they could establish some connexion with the rather pathetic and very poorly paid group of ribbon-weavers they might be able to help them, for example, by putting them into touch with the makers of looms and shuttles in England who have lately learnt these crafts in response to the new demands. The old makers, on whom the Coventry weavers used to rely, have all died out, so that when these women need repairs to a loom, or a new shuttle, they have to make shift with what they can cobble up for themselves, or what the factory can supply. The shuttles which the factory can obtain for them are not suited to the work because the factory is only in touch with the manufacturers of accessories for power-looms, who do not understand the needs of the hand-loom weaver. It is possible, also, that the modern weaving industries, with their outlet to new markets, might be able to turn to account the knowledge and skill of these old workers, the demand for the product of whose looms is now so small from their regular employers that there is not enough work to keep busy even the small number who remain.

Another point of importance with regard to the chances of success for new weaving industries is that a market must be ' felt for ' and connexions with customers built up gradually. A weaver may be tempted to sink all her capital in apparatus and material and start off enthusiastically to work on orders from friends, which will perhaps keep her busy for some months, at the end of which period she may find that these people, being supplied, can give her no more orders for a long time and may even, if she has not perfected herself in the craft and has turned out meanwhile faulty and too loosely woven materials, forsake her altogether. In the same way, an industry started from philanthropic motives to give employment to the disabled may collapse when the original organizer, who perhaps had special facilities for disposing of the work, leaves it to be carried on by the workers alone, who have no outlet for their goods nor means of finding one.

viii. *Notes on Mat-Weaving.*

The weaving of mats on hand-looms is carried on in many institutions for the blind and by individual blinded men in various towns and villages, often together with basket-making and other crafts. Small factories or workshops are also found in which this work only is done, or the weaving may be an adjunct to the business of rope-making. Two firms of this last kind were visited in the south-eastern counties ; one, which also made ropes and trugs, had thirty hand-looms for the weaving of mats, although only four of them were being worked in 1922 ; the other firm has already been referred to as one which used to carry on the weaving of ' sails ' and hop-pockets by hand, but which, since the war, has used hand-looms only for mat-making. Other mat factories are usually to be found in urban districts, and here, as elsewhere, there is evidence of the precarious condition into which the industry seems to have fallen recently, owing to foreign competition, similar mats being made more cheaply by hand in India.

The looms are similar to those used in ordinary hand-loom weaving, but of stouter build and with very heavy battens. The process is that of hand-weaving, with variations, akin to the method of weaving velvet by hand. The pile is formed by threading short lengths of fibre under the warp or, in the case of large, rough mats, by picking up one weft thread of yarn in a loop between each thread of the warp and shearing through the loops with a knife, leaving the ends upstanding. Such work is not very skilled.

The laborious processes of unwinding the skeins of yarn for splicing the ends (which is done by out-workers), and of rewinding the ' pads ' (heaps of yarn) into balls, could be equally well carried out by machinery, and are indeed done in this way in some factories. Probably the cheapness of out-workers' labour in some places such as the colliery town of Pontefract, where there are many miners' wives who are glad to earn a little money by a home occupation, would make the introduction of machinery for unwinding the bales unnecessary in the factory here. But the work is dreary, monotonous, and poorly paid, the number of women employed is not great, and, although they would undoubtedly miss the small monetary benefit which they derive from it, their employment cannot be viewed with any enthusiasm, nor can the probable cessation of it be considered as a disaster.

As regards the St. Dunstan's mat-makers, these men have generally settled in their native places, regardless of whether these are suitable centres for the industry, but as they often supplement mat-making with boot-repairing or basket-making and, in any case, are less dependent on the industry than on their pensions for a livelihood, they are not important figures in a survey of rural industries. They probably make only a few mats from time to time for the orders of local people who wish to contribute to their support.

The institutions for the blind also receive orders from regular customers, many of whom need mats made in special sizes, but foreign competition is felt by these workers. The simplicity of the apparatus and processes employed suggest that the industry would be a suitable one for a country district and for workers engaged in some other part-time occupation. The making of mats of various kinds has already been mentioned as a side-line to an ordinary hand-loom weaving industry, and in this case, again, individual orders for special sizes could be executed. But the condition of the industry when it was investigated in 1921 and 1922 did not point to any likelihood of future development, but rather to its speedy decline.

CHAPTER III

LACE-MAKING

i. *Lace-Making Districts.*

LACE-MAKING survives as a cottage industry, carried on
by part-time workers, throughout a large area of the East
Midlands, in many villages of East Devon, centring round
Honiton and Exeter, and, to a smaller extent, in Coggeshall
and one or two adjacent villages in Essex. Isolated individual
workers are also found in other districts but they are either
migrants from one of these areas or else have learnt the craft
as a hobby ; they are not really representative of the industry.
In the Honiton district and the East Midlands the majority
of the present workers are the descendants of an unbroken
line of lace-makers who have carried on the industry through
many vicissitudes for hundreds of years. The Coggeshall
lace industry is of more recent origin. The rise of the lace
industry in England was probably due to the Flemish
Protestant exiles who, fleeing from the persecution of
Philip II of Spain in the Low Countries, came in 1563 to
Kent. It is recorded that amongst them were a number of
makers of ' bone-lace ', so called through the use of bone
bobbins, or, possibly, the use of bones, sharpened, for pins.
In 1567, when a further persecution drove more Flemings
over, they began to spread to the Midlands ; in 1568 they
had made their way to Cranfield, Beds., and later came to
Newport Pagnell, Olney, and Buckingham. They brought
with them their lace-pillows, bobbins, and parchment patterns
and seem to have taught the craft to many people. The
industry spread rapidly and widely and bobbin lace was much
in demand throughout the seventeenth and well into the
eighteenth century. The Ripon and Norwich districts and
the counties of Wilts. and Somerset have all been famous as
centres of lace-making, in addition to the areas in which it
still survives. Towards the end of the eighteenth century,
however, the use of lace became more restricted and in many
districts the industry flagged and died out.

The original bobbin lace was, of course, made of linen
thread and was of a coarser type than the present Point
Ground or Buckingham lace. This was introduced at the

end of the eighteenth century and continued in popularity until 1851. In this year Maltese lace was shown at the Great Exhibition and took the public fancy. The lacemakers of the Midlands found it easy to learn to make this lace, which could be turned out quicker than the native kinds, so they endeavoured by turning their attention to this new kind and by using the cheaper cotton instead of linen thread, to compete with the machine-made lace which was becoming increasingly popular. Frames for making point nets by machine first appeared at Mansfield as early as 1786, and in 1808 and 1809 patents were taken out for improved methods of making bobbin net. For at least thirty years before this thousands of women had been employed in and around Nottingham to embroider ornaments on net. In 1813 figured net-weaving machines were considerably improved and, as a result, lace-making machines were rapidly developed.

The making of Maltese lace does not seem to have been taken up in the Honiton district, and, in consequence, the industry there has suffered a steady decline since the beginning of the nineteenth century. But in the Midlands there was a temporary boom following 1851 until the competition of factory-made lace became so serious as to cause a rapid reduction in the wages earned by the hand-workers. Their earnings became so low that by about 1880 few of them found that lace was worth making, the pillows were laid aside, and mothers no longer taught their daughters the craft. Most of the lace schools had died out about 1870, being replaced by the elementary schools founded under the new Education Act, in which no lace-making was taught.

Coggeshall lace is also of Continental origin, but was introduced into England far more recently than pillow-lace, late enough for the effects of the industrial revolution to prevent it from spreading very widely, although it attained to a certain prosperity in a limited area. About the year 1820 a Huguenot refugee settled in Coggeshall with his two daughters. The girls were skilled in the art of making Tambour Lace, so called from the fact that the net, which forms the groundwork of the lace, was stretched over a round frame, like that of a tambourine, whilst the design was embroidered on it with a crotchet hook. The industry took root and increased in Coggeshall and a few neighbouring villages, and one of the 'tambour-masters' took some workers over to Limerick in 1849 and established tambour lace-making there. At one time there were many of these

' tambour-masters ', or dealers in lace, in the Coggeshall
district, but now only two remain, and as there has been no
organized teaching of the craft since the closing of the schools
or workrooms in which children were taught from the age
of eight, the industry is likely to die out.

In the Midlands, cases of men making lace are recorded,
but these were probably men who were disqualified by
age or infirmity for agricultural or other active work. The
workers have consisted almost exclusively of the women of
the farm labourer's family, from the child of six or seven
to her grandmother or great-grandmother.

The bobbin lace industry at present extends over parts of
the counties of Huntingdon, Northampton, Bedford, Buckingham, Oxford, and East Devon. In Huntingdonshire it is
chiefly found in the south of the county, along the Bedfordshire border, and the total number of lace-makers in the
county is very few. The South Hunts. Lace-Making Association has only two workers who make any regular quantity
of lace and the numerous buyers found in other counties
are lacking here. Bedfordshire contains a great number of
workers, but there are fewer to the south-east of Bedford and
to the south of Ampthill than in the rest of the county. In
Bedford there are shops which sell the lace and there are
also private buyers. The chief lace-making district of
Northamptonshire is the eastern part of the county, around
the villages of Yardley Hastings, Denton, and Hackleton,
and further west, around Towcester. In Buckinghamshire
the industry centres chiefly around Olney, where are found
many buyers and dealers, pattern designers and prickers,
and others interested in the craft. Newport Pagnell, Stoke
Goldington, Weston Underwood, and other villages in this
district are famous for their lace-makers. The industry
as found in the more western part of the county, around
Buckingham, and also in the Thame district of Oxfordshire,
has been dealt with elsewhere.[1] In South Buckinghamshire
the industry is also carried on round High Wycombe,
Princes Risborough, and Aylesbury, but it seems to be less
firmly established there, where it was a later growth and has
been less well organized recently. The lace made here is
chiefly of the Maltese variety and is, on the whole, of inferior
quality, but it is sold by retailers at rates which are rather
higher than in the north of the county and in Bedfordshire,
although the workers do not earn more. A few isolated

[1] *The Rural Industries round Oxford.* K. S. Woods (Clarendon Press).

makers of bobbin lace were found in other counties, but they have little connexion with the industry of the Midlands and of Devonshire.

It is impossible to estimate the number of workers now regularly making lace. The census returns for Bedfordshire give the numbers as 6,728 in 1861 ; 4,792 in 1881 ; and 1,148 in 1901. Since 1901 there seems to have been a slight decrease, but this may be due to changes in the categories in which the lace-makers now appear.

The kinds of lace known as 'Bedford' and 'Buckingham' respectively, are both made in all of the East Midland counties, and it is not clear why they have received these names. The Buckingham, or 'point ground', is the older variety in this district, many of the designs having been introduced in the time of Charles II by Flemish immigrants from Brussels, Mechlin, and Valenciennes. The Bedford lace includes the more recently introduced Maltese, Torchon, and Cluny patterns, which have been copied from those made in the places after which they are named. There is a tendency for certain kinds of work to be found in certain villages, as 'linen-work', or Cluny lace, at Stevington (Beds.), 'yard lace' of the Maltese kind at Stoke Goldington (Bucks.), and 'point ground' at Yardley Hastings (Bucks.), but, except for this, no distribution of the different kinds over special areas can be noted.

ii. *Varieties, Materials, and Apparatus.*

In Honiton lace, known as Honiton Point or Stitch, there is to be seen a development of bobbin lace similar to a kind still made in Belgium, known as Brussels lace, but not found in the Midlands. Separate 'sprigs' of this lace are made up on the pillow and are then put together in the form of a collar, or edging, or whatever is required, by a woman known as the 'pointer'. She used to fill in the spaces between the sprigs with a needle, but this groundwork is now more usually done with the bobbins on a pillow. This method of lace-making may be compared with that introduced recently at Paulerspury, in Northants., where sprigs of pillow-lace were sewn on to net, in this case machine-made, with the object of diminishing the cost of large pieces of lace by having only the 'sprigs' made by hand. There are three grades of Honiton lace. The best and finest, called 'raised work', is almost dying out amongst the older workers although it is successfully taught to children in the County

Council lace classes. The other kinds are distinguished by
the workers as ' second-best ' and ' plain '.

The Point Ground or Buckingham lace is worked in ' half-
stitch ', i. e. two bobbins to a pin. It should be made of fine
linen thread but it is often worked with cotton. It is a much
finer sort of lace than Maltese and the making of it slow work.
One of the simplest patterns of a narrow edging can be
worked with nine pairs of bobbins. The ' Fan ', another
of the simpler patterns, takes forty bobbins. Wider and
more elaborate patterns sometimes require from four hundred
to six hundred bobbins, and collars and other large pieces
of work need sometimes as many as seven hundred. When
such numbers are used they are tied together in bundles
to keep them out of the way, only the group manipulated
for the moment being left free.

The patterns for point ground lace have a great many
pin-holes set very close together, so that to work this lace,
especially in an unfamiliar pattern, is trying to the eyes.
Some of the older workers find the finest patterns beyond
their ability for this reason. In fact, there are very few
lace-makers left who can or will make the most elaborate
and delicate of the old patterns. There are also few workers
now who can make the wide collars, which are more difficult
to work than the straight ' yard lace '. The making of point
ground lace tends, on the whole, to die out because it is more
skilled, slower, and less remunerative work than the making
of the coarser kinds.

Bedford lace, generally made of cotton thread, is done in
' whole-stitch ', i. e. four bobbins to a pin. In the making
of Buckingham lace there are two bobbins to each pin, so
that in Bedford lace more threads have to be twisted between
each pin, and this kind is therefore stronger and coarser and,
since the pin-holes in the patterns are not so close together,
more quickly made. This lace is made in the form of straight
edgings, or ' yard lace ', both wide and narrow square
borders for handkerchiefs, tray cloths, &c., ' motives ', i. e.
small pieces of lace in a butterfly, flower or other design,
used for trimming blouses or underclothing ; and in square
pieces used for nightdress cases. The Maltese and Torchon
patterns are used for all these purposes, while the Cluny
or linen work is chiefly made into tray-cloth borders. About
fifty years ago a kind of lace called ' Yak ', made of black
wool, was very popular and very remunerative to make.
Maltese and Torchon patterns may be made in silk thread
or ' Sylko '.

BUCKINGHAM LACE

Reproduced by kind permission of the Curators of the Victoria and Albert Museum

HONITON LACE

Reproduced by kind permission of the Curators of the Victoria and Albert Museum

At Paulerspury (Northants.) the wife of a former vicar introduced the making of wide collars, or ' berthas ', and veils of net with tiny flower motives of point ground lace *appliqué* to the net. This lady did a great deal to revive the industry in this district and sold much of the work among her friends whilst she remained in the parish. The industry has now been dropped. The flower motives were specially designed or else taken from old patterns of wide lace. The designing and pricking of the parchments was done by a woman in the village. Many different workers made the lace, and another one sewed the lace on to the net. A narrow lace border was pricked out from an old pattern, worked, and sewn on to edge the veil or collar. Since the net was the ordinary machine-made material, a cheaper article was produced by sewing the small pieces of lace on to this than could have been possible if the whole thing had been of hand-worked lace. Hundreds of tiny ' motives ' were sometimes used on a big veil or scarf, and the sewing on of them was very delicate work. Sometimes the net was cut away beneath them. The co-operative element in the work seems to have been stimulating to the workers, who speak with pride of the elaborate pieces produced by their united labour.

The different parts of a piece of lace on the pillow are known as the foot-side or straight edge, by which the lace is to be sewn on, the ground work or centre part, and the head side or outer edge. The foot-side has more threads twisted into it to give extra strength, and the head-side also has more thickly set pins. Thus there is relatively more work in the two edges than in the ground work and so a wider lace is more economical of time.

The patterns for yard lace are generally made in strips of one-third of a yard long. This strip is pinned on to the pillow and the lace-maker works down the whole length of it. She then has to remove all the pins, roll up the strip of lace, and start at the top of the parchment again. The piece of lace worked on the length of the parchment is known as the ' down ' and workers will often measure their output as ' a down a day '. In a very wide and elaborate pattern the whole design may not be complete in twelve inches and the parchment is longer, sometimes as much as twenty-two inches long.

' Lace thread ' (cotton) is sold in quarter-ounce parcels, each containing a number of ' slips ', the number varying according to the fineness of the thread. ' Twelve-slip ', one of the finer sorts, which is used for many point ground patterns, costs 1s. 10½d. a parcel.[1]

It is very difficult to obtain from a worker any estimate as to the amount of thread used to make a yard of lace, but where lace classes are held the thread is usually provided by the teacher, who charges the children for it at the rate of a halfpenny per yard of lace made, so this may be taken as the average cost for the simpler patterns of the narrow edgings. Another worker reckoned the average cost at 1d. a yard for coarse, and 2d. a yard for fine work, in edgings two or three inches wide.

Linen thread, which is used particularly for Cluny patterns, costs 4s. a lb., and one worker estimated that a wide border one yard square, representing two or three weeks' work, and for which she would be paid 22s., would require a quarter of a pound of thread.

The price of the thread may be estimated at from 3½ to 4½ per cent. of the price obtained for the work by the Midland lace-makers, but it will, of course, vary with the kind of thread used. One worker, who charges for her lace on a basis of 3d. an hour for the time spent on it, adds to this an extra 1d. per hour for the cost of thread, which is nearly always provided by the worker except when special orders are executed.

'Parchments', as the patterns for the Bedford and Buckingham lace are always called, are nowadays often pricked out on pasteboard. The parchment itself is made at a factory at Newport Pagnell. The parchment patterns are, on the whole, preferred by the lace-makers, although, when new, they are more difficult to stick the pins into, and the worker's fingers frequently become sore. But the genuine parchments last much longer than the pasteboard patterns. In fact, there are in existence thousands of old patterns which must have been used dozens, perhaps hundreds, of times, and thousands more were destroyed during the worst times of the industry. A new pasteboard 'parchment' costs from a shilling upwards. For a particular pattern of insertion one inch wide in point ground the pasteboard parchment, twelve inches long, costs 1s. 3d. and the genuine parchment 1s. 9d.

The various lace-making associations use old patterns chiefly, but several buyers and dealers make their own designs, or adapt old ones. Some of the ancient patterns

---

[1] All figures of prices and wages for the Midlands were collected in 1923, and for the Honiton district in 1920.

which do not exist in many examples are much valued, and occasionally at a sale of the effects of some descendant of the old buyers a hoard of these now much sought after patterns may be found stowed away in a forgotten box. Many of the well-known patterns, such as the Fan, Cat-face, Butterfly, and Running River, exist in thousands of replicas.

The design of the lace is of the greatest importance, especially in the finer and more elaborate varieties, and an old worker may sometimes obtain a particularly good price for a piece of lace worked from an old and little-known pattern which she happens to have in her possession.

The designing and pricking of the patterns is very skilled work and is done by special ' prickers '. A few of the best lace-makers can prick a new parchment by pinning the strip of card under the strip they are working from, and so pricking through from one to the other. But there is a danger of duplicating any errors which may occur in the old pattern through a pin having been stuck in carelessly. After pricking, certain lines have to be marked on the parchment in ink to guide the worker and this is the process in which some women, who could achieve the pricking, fail. Yet this pricking and marking of a new pattern from an old must be a fairly simple process, and the inability of the workers to do it for themselves illustrates their inadaptability, which may be partly due to the fact that in many cases the only education a lace-maker received was at the lace-school, where she learnt little but the technique of lace-making and that often by crude methods.

There are a few women designers and prickers of patterns, who may or may not be lace-makers themselves. A man who cannot make lace may be able to design patterns, if he thoroughly understands how the lace is worked. The design for a piece of lace is drawn first on white cardboard. This requires great concentration, as the designer must bear in mind all the time the movements of each bobbin as the lace will be worked, lest the worker be led into an *impasse* and get the bobbins so grouped that the work cannot be continued without breaking off a bunch of threads and starting again. After the pattern has been drawn on the card it is pricked through on to brown pasteboard and the guiding lines inked in. Many teachers of lace-making consider that the children should be taught to design and prick their own patterns, but others say that if this rule is adhered to it will prevent the children from learning to make point ground lace, as the pricking of the patterns for this, except in the case of the most elementary designs, is too difficult for them. Others hold that the child should first become thoroughly proficient in the making of lace and might then learn how to make the patterns. The idea of teaching the pattern-pricking side by side with the making of lace seems, however, to be a step in the right direction, as tending to develop the child's mind to a greater extent.

Amongst the Honiton lace-makers the designing and pricking of patterns seems to be work requiring less skill. Each lace-maker works her small sprigs at random, not designing them with a view to the particular piece of lace of which they are ultimately to form a part. These sprigs are bought up by dealers, and the pointer may have to contrive her ' set-pieces ' from a number of differing scraps collected from scattered makers. In putting them together she often imitates some ancient pattern, which may be good in itself but cannot lend to its modern copy the homogeneity which is necessary to a work of art. The sprigs and pointing themselves are often very poor in design and a good deal of coarse and inferior work is done, although there are still some lace-makers whose workmanship is excellent. The standard of work is said to have deteriorated during the war owing to the difficulty of obtaining the fine thread from Nottingham. Amongst the older workers there seem to be no such expert designers as there are in the Midlands, and the pattern of the sprigs is usually so simple that any worker can, without special training, prick out a new design for herself, copying it from the wall-paper or from any design she comes across. As a result of these casual methods, both of designing and of putting together, Honiton lace has deteriorated considerably.

The pillows are bolster shaped and stuffed tightly with straw. In the Midlands there are a few men who make these pillows in their spare time and who supply them wholesale to the shops which sell lace, where the workers can obtain them. Very often a girl who takes up lace-making can obtain an old discarded pillow from her mother or grandmother. A ' horse ', or three-legged wooden stool, is also needed on which to place the pillow. A firm of linen manufacturers have produced a French pillow of an improved type. It is smaller than that in common use and is made on a wooden reel, turning on an axle into a square opening in the centre of a wooden tray. On this pillow the worker does not have to unpin the work continually and ' set up ' again at the top of the pillow ; but merely removes the pattern when she has

KINDS, MATERIALS, AND APPARATUS 59

worked to the end of it and places it again under the work
at the point where it leaves off, turning the pillow round
on its axle. These pillows cost about 5s. Only one of the
twenty or thirty lace-makers visited used one, and she was
a woman of better education than the average worker.

Bobbin winders are little wooden devices for winding the
thread on to the bobbins. No change from the traditional
pattern has been introduced by the present makers. It was
stated that a few village carpenters still make winders, but
no instances were found. Generally the winder in use had
been in the lace-maker's family as long as any one could
remember. They are also supplied by firms which make
a speciality of bobbin lace apparatus.

The bobbins are of bone or wood, turned and often carved,
inlaid with pewter or brass, painted, or wound with brass
wire. Some have names or mottoes carved or painted on
them, while others are specimens of very skilled carving,
such as the 'church window' design, carved with a 'lantern'
in the middle, inside which is a tiny bobbin, detached, but
all cut out of the same piece of wood. The ordinary turned
wooden bobbins used to be sold at 2d. a dozen. Many years
ago, when there were from fifty to a hundred lace-makers in
some villages, pedlars sold the bobbins from door to door.
A bobbin was often given to a child in a lace school as
a reward when her first piece of lace was completed, and the
lads of the village carved bobbins for their girls. Nowadays
old bobbins can be bought in many shops in the lace-making
districts, prices varying according to the workmanship and
also according to the estimated status of the buyer. On the
end of each bobbin there are about half a dozen coloured
beads threaded on a wire loop, called the 'spangles', which
serve to weight the bobbin and thus to keep it flat on the
pillow in its place. Workers often used to buy the plain
bobbins and spangle them for themselves.

It was estimated by a lace teacher that the initial outlay
on bobbins, pillow, &c., would be from 10s. to 15s., if the
worker had none of the apparatus in her possession. The
equipment of the old lace schools [1] included, in addition to
the apparatus mentioned, the candle-stool—a stool on which
a candle or rush-light was set, the light shining through four
glass flasks filled with water, set on wooden posts around
the candle. The light was magnified by the water in the
flasks to such an extent that twelve women could work by
the light of one candle. This device might well be adopted

[1] See A. A. Carnes, *Bedfordshire Hand-made Lace*.

to-day by the many women who work at handicrafts in ill-lit rooms in country cottages. The flasks, when not in use, were kept in 'hutches', or rush baskets.

Coggeshall or Tambour lace is worked upon a foundation of fine net which is no longer stretched in the old round 'tambour' frame, but across an oblong framework. The pattern is worked in chain-stitch on the net, beneath which the thread from the spool is passed by the worker's left hand and is drawn through the meshes of the net with the crotchet hook held in her right hand above.

iii. *Organization.*

Within the last twenty years a number of organizations have been formed, chiefly in the Midlands, with the object of reviving, or preventing the extinction of, the lace industry, and of assisting the workers to obtain as good prices as possible. The lace-makers are said to have been much exploited by buyers before the organizations were formed, with the result that only women in the direst poverty would make lace, while the quality tended to deteriorate and the whole industry was in danger of dying out. These societies in the Midlands aim at encouraging the use of the best patterns and usually they take some part in the planning of classes in lace-making. The chief of them and the scope of their work are described here in outline, since the comparatively alive and flourishing condition of the lace industry in this district is largely due to their activities and is in considerable contrast to the condition of the Coggeshall and Honiton industries.

The Huntingdonshire Pillow Lace Association was formed about twenty years ago. Subscriptions of 5s. each were collected from a number of residents in the county and the association bought quantities of old parchments, pillows, bobbins, and winders from families in which these were no longer used. Some members of the Association learnt the craft and taught many village women to make both the point ground and torchon laces. The Association bought up lace from the workers and resold it to friends and other customers with whom they got into touch privately. They have tried to encourage the formation of lace classes in connexion with the elementary schools, and through their endeavours a considerable number of the younger generation have become fairly proficient, but very few of these now practise the craft and there seems to have been much less

LACE MAKERS OLD AND YOUNG

Reproduced by kind permission of Miss C. L. F. Dalton

of a revival in this county than elsewhere. The Association has paid its way from the beginning. In selling lace, about 1*d.* per yard is added to the price paid to the workers, and there is no difficulty in disposing of all the lace made, but the sales cannot be pushed because the supply is a very uncertain one and reliance cannot be placed on the execution of an order within any given time.

The Bedford Lace Education Committee was formed mainly to promote the teaching of lace-making, although it also buys the lace when the workers desire this. There are, however, so many other buyers in this county that this is not such a necessary function of the Association as in the case of Huntingdonshire, although the fact that it is always ready to buy good lace at a certain rate of payment helps to keep the rates paid by other buyers nearly up to that standard. Lace-makers generally say that the Association pays rather more than most of the shops or travelling buyers. The Committee works in collaboration with the County Council Education Committee and has received a County Council grant since 1907. A few years ago this amounted to £90, in 1922 it was £35, and £55 was applied for in 1923. The grant is chiefly spent on teachers' fees. Some special classes are held for training teachers. The Committee sends most of the lace which it buys to the Anglo-Belgian Lace Industries shop in London, also known as the ' Beds. and Bucks. Depot '.

The North Bucks. Lace Association was founded in 1897 for the purpose of reviving the lace industry, more especially the making of point ground lace, and to facilitate the sale of the lace, eliminating, so far as possible, the middleman's profits. Lace is sold through the Beds. and Bucks. Depot and classes are organized to teach the point ground variety. The Association was at first run by voluntary workers, but its increasing scope has necessitated the employment of paid workers who collect the lace, often give out patterns to be made for special orders, and supply the thread to the workers to ensure the use of the best material.

The Midland Lace Association has its head-quarters in Northampton and works chiefly in that county. This Association does not organize classes. There seems to be an unfortunate failure on the part of this body and of the ' Northampton Lace School ' (see below) to collaborate effectively with the County Council, who annually vote a grant for the encouragement of the lace industry, which is seldom used through the failure of any organization to put

62 LACE-MAKING

in a claim for it backed by any acceptable scheme. No paid staff is employed by this Association. A small shop is maintained in Northampton where the lace which is brought in by the workers is sold. A percentage is added to the cost of the lace, sufficient to cover overhead expenses.

The Northampton Lace School is an organization formed by two ladies, one of whom takes a great interest in the revival and support of the lace industry. One of the partners teaches girls in Northampton to embroider and their work is bought by the shop. The other partner gives some private lessons in lace-making, but, as far as the lace industry is concerned, this organization is really only a centre for buying lace from the workers for sale in the shop.

Both in Devonshire and in the Midland counties a number of classes are held under the auspices of the County Council Education Committee for instructing elementary school children and adults in the designing and working of the native bobbin lace. In some of the Midland counties the authorities have not always been agreed as to the desirability or usefulness of these classes and some of them have been discontinued. In Huntingdonshire lace-making was taught in five schools from 1904 until about 1917. But the craft seems to have lost its foothold in this county some time ago, little interest being taken in it by the villages, and, in the interests of economy, the classes have been dropped. In Bedfordshire classes have been held since 1907. They generally take place on Saturday mornings and are optional for children of from seven years up to a few years over school age. The pupils either pay 6d. a term and are supplied with patterns and materials, or else the classes are free and the children pay for the actual materials supplied to them. They generally bring their own pillows and bobbins, but these are, if necessary, sold to them by the teacher. The class may consist of from seven to twelve members, and it is stated that the full number generally attend. There seems to be a tendency among the children to fall off as they grow older. There have, however, been several requests from adults for classes, and the Lace Education Committee is anxious to try to meet these, especially as it becomes increasingly difficult to obtain efficient teachers.

The classes are now being organized in accordance with the Belgian method of teaching. The series of text books and pattern cards known as *Les Dentelles aux fuseaux*[1] is used, as there are no similar English instruction books. The

[1] Published by the *Bibliothèque D.M.C.*, Th. de Dillmont, Editeur, Mulhouse, France.

diagrams in this series are very clear and enable the children to learn to prick their own patterns as they learn the stitches. The torchon patterns are first learnt, as these are the easiest, and they are used as a basis from which to lead up to the point ground patterns. A local honorary manager is responsible for the organization of the classes and a paid teacher gives the instruction. The classes are primarily intended for school children, but it is expected that some of the older girls who are allowed to join may later be trained as teachers.

In Northamptonshire a few classes were held in 1911, but there seem to have been none since then owing to the unfortunate position there.

Various difficulties are encountered by the organizers of lace classes held in school buildings after school hours. For instance, it is seldom that a class of even the minimum number can be got together out of school hours during the summer months, whilst from October until the spring, when the children would be willing to attend, the lighting of the class-room is a difficulty. Good light is more needed by learners than by experienced workers who know the patterns, and the teacher also needs a good light by which to examine the work. Then, too, teachers generally dislike holding a Saturday class. In Northamptonshire the grants are only given for evening classes for children over school age and for adults, and at least twenty hours' instruction must be given. £3 is granted towards the cost of a class and any further expenses must be defrayed locally. These regulations have probably proved stumbling-blocks to some would-be organizers of classes.

As stated already, it is very difficult now to find competent teachers. The present generation of lace-makers learnt from women who were very skilled in the craft, but had little or no education, and although their standard was high and they insisted on the production of good work, yet many of them had the crudest ideas of teaching. They would set a child to work out a hard pattern with little or no explanation, and although the pupil eventually attained to a considerable degree of skill, it was only after many hours of misery. Organizers of classes say that it is very noticeable that the daughters of lace-makers learn more quickly than others and consider that there is a certain inherited skill in the craft which should not be allowed to die out. But, though this may be true, it is also clear that a child who had watched her mother or any one else making lace would have some idea of how to set about the work and so would naturally

64   LACE-MAKING

learn more quickly than another to whom the whole process
was unfamiliar. Learners attain proficiency in the fan-
pattern, the first one taught in point ground lace, in from
one to four lessons of one hour each.

There is a considerable amount of skill needed to make
good lace, apart from the mere ability to make the stitches
and follow the pattern. The bobbins must be pulled tight
enough or the work will be too loose of texture and soon wear
out of shape, but if a fine thread is used it is easily snapped
if the bobbin is pulled too sharply. The use of the finer
threads tends to develop in the worker a greater delicacy of
touch and sureness of manipulation. A good teacher must
be a thoroughly skilled lace-maker and also have a good
understanding of the whole theory and practice of pattern
designing and pricking, in addition to the ability to teach.
Undoubtedly, in the anxiety to revive the industry, incom-
petent teachers have been employed, so that the children
have turned out poor work, and, when they tried to sell their
lace, and have been unable to do so, they have been discouraged. The idea that the craft can only be adequately
acquired at the early age of five or six is simply rooted in
conservatism. Adults can learn quickly and become skilled
workers, especially if they are good needlewomen or have
any natural capacity for delicate hand-work.

Although in Devonshire the lace-making industry does
not seem to have been revived to the same extent as in the
Midlands, although the voluntary organizations, which have,
in the latter district, done so much to effect this revival, are
lacking, and although the workers do not seem to have been
brought into touch with any steady outside market for their
work, yet the teaching of lace-making is being carried on
with enthusiasm. When the investigation was made (1921),
there were fourteen lace classes supervised by a County
Council teacher specially employed for the purpose. This
teacher, herself a native of Honiton, is making, under the
guidance of the Exeter School of Art, very beautiful designs,
inspired by old lace but not imitating it, and without the
over-elaboration that has helped to spoil the market for
Honiton lace. The children who attend the classes are
encouraged to make, in their spare time, drawings of wild
flowers which may be suitable for adaptation to designs for
lace. It is hoped that thus, by the infusion of an element
of freshness combined with simplicity into the designs, the
Honiton lace industry will be truly ' revived ', even though
there seems to be little market for the work. Twelve of

these lace classes are attended by elementary school children and two by adults. There are eight pupils in a class, who attend for two hours each week, the girls usually from ten years of age until they leave school. In this time they learn a great number of patterns and fillings, and although nearly all of them go into service on leaving school and most of them give up lace-making, yet a few continue the work and keep in touch with the lace teacher. The classes have been held for about sixteen years, so that by now there must be in the district a number of skilled lace-makers between the ages of twenty and thirty, who may possibly take up the work again when they are older.

In the Coggeshall district there is an association called the Coggeshall Tambour Lace-workers, formed in 1910. The aims and scope of this society can only be inferred, because the promoters were unwilling to give information. From the evidence of people in the neighbourhood, it seems clear that the association, which buys up lace for re-sale, has almost doubled the earnings of the makers, by raising the standard of payment and finding a more extensive market. There seems, however, to have been no attempt here to teach the craft of lace-making to any of the younger generation, and, in fact, the association is often criticized in the neighbourhood for its failure to organize classes.

iv. *Markets.*

There seems to be a ready sale for almost all kinds of lace made in the Midlands, but especially for the best, finest and most elaborate point ground work, which is becoming very rare. Probably if all workers made this it could not be disposed of, as it is very expensive and the market must be a limited one, but at present the demand for this type of lace exceeds the supply. It seems to be less easy to dispose quickly of the cheaper and coarser kinds, such as the Maltese and Torchon edgings, probably because many people prefer the better kinds of machine-made lace which can be bought at the same price. There is also a good cheap supply of these varieties from the Continent and from China. The borders for tray- and table-cloths in Cluny or linen work are popular, and the smaller and less expensive pieces of point ground, such as narrow edgings and handkerchief borders, are generally easily disposed of. In Devonshire it was said that the demand for the best work was falling off, and most of the lace is sold to tourists, who buy the smallest and cheapest pieces.

This striking difference of affairs as regards the demand for lace in these two districts can probably be explained by the fact that in the Midlands the sale is effected chiefly through various organizations which are able to reach a wide circle of customers through the private acquaintances of many of the persons who have interested themselves in the revival of the industry. Their success in disposing of the lace has probably stimulated the ordinary dealers to seek markets further afield, and several of them supply certain London shops.

A number of firms, chiefly drapers and ' art needlework ' shops, in Bedfordshire, Northants., and Bucks., make a speciality of stocking the lace of the district. There are two such shops in Bedford and several in South Buckinghamshire. They also sell parchments, bobbins, and pillows, to the workers. In some cases they send buyers round the villages and in others the workers bring the lace in to them. From the fact that they seem anxious to obtain as much lace as possible it may be inferred that they make a good profit on it.

In addition to these buyers there are, particularly in Buckinghamshire and Bedfordshire, a number of men who visit the villages to buy lace, which they sell to private customers and to a few big London shops.

In Devonshire the chief sale for the lace seems to be through a shop in Honiton, the proprietress of which, herself a skilled lace-maker, has for many years done valuable work, not only in providing the lace-makers with a market, but also in encouraging the finer work, supplying prickings from better designs than those commonly in use, and generally supervising the designing and pricking. She has collectors in many villages who buy the sprigs from the workers, but she does not find it easy to dispose of the better work. There are a number of other dealers, and village shops used to accumulate an embarrassing amount of Honiton sprigs and lace in payment of debts for groceries and other necessities. There are still traces of payment for the lace in kind. It is not likely that local dealers make a big profit out of the lace, though successful businesses have been built up. But since there is so little sale for the most expensive pieces of lace the dealers cannot take the risk of expending large sums of money upon such pieces, which they might not be able to dispose of for a long time, if at all. In the Midlands, on the other hand, those dealers with wider connexions are only too pleased when they come across a worker who is able

and willing to make one of the big elaborate patterns in the
finest point ground, which takes many months to do. This
kind of work is only done to order, but there seems to be no
scarcity of orders for it. In Devon a few of these large pieces
of work have been done to order for church linen and wedding
veils. The collectors for the Honiton lace shop receive 1d. in
1s. commission, and the workers have the advantage of being
paid in cash.

In the Coggeshall district there are now only two dealers
or 'tambour masters', in addition to the 'Coggeshall
Tambour Lace-workers', the association already mentioned.
Much of the Coggeshall lace is sold through the Home Arts
and Industries and the Englishwoman Exhibitions, and
some of the individual workers sell through the exhibitions
organized by the Women's Institutes, as do also the Midland
lace-makers in a few cases. There does not seem to be any
sale for the lace through the ordinary commercial channels.
This may be partly owing to the fact that the dealers make
very little attempt to adapt the designs to the modern
market. Collars of old-fashioned pattern are still made,
and other large pieces, whereas smaller 'motives' for use
as trimmings might command a better sale. Coggeshall
lace is, by its nature, unsuited for making up as 'yard
lace' and edgings, which are, perhaps, the most generally
popular forms.

v. *The Workers and their Earnings.*

The variations in earnings and the difficulty in estimating
the average rates of pay are very great. All the makers are
part-time workers, and many of them are aged and sometimes
crippled and in feeble health. Others, however, are young
or middle-aged women in good health, but all of them find
it difficult to give any idea of the number of hours during
which they sit at the pillow, and even if they know this
they do not say how many times during those hours a kettle
boiled over or a child's cry warned its mother that it demanded
her instant attention. It is impossible to work for many
hours at a time at the very finest patterns, and after a couple
of hours a rest for nearly as long again may be needed. It
was noticeable, however, that the majority of workers visited
at any hour of the day between 10 a.m. and 5 p.m. were
found at work unless they were at dinner. A member of one
of the Associations estimated that most women earned from
2d. to 3d. an hour, but some would work for 1d. an hour.

A young married woman of considerable intelligence, who
has taught lace-making and is one of the best of the younger
makers of point ground lace, said that her own estimate of
the amount she could earn was 1½*d*. an hour.

It is generally admitted that it is quite impossible to earn
a livelihood by lace-making. One expert worker, who had
to support herself entirely, had given up this work in favour
of plain and fancy needlework, not because she could not
dispose of the lace, but because it was not possible to earn
by it enough to live.

In Devonshire the pre-war earnings could not have been
more than 1*d*. or 2*d*. an hour, and since the war they seem to
average from 3*d*. to 4*d*. an hour. For the raised work, which
takes longer, a good worker can earn rather more than for
the plain. It is noticeable that two makers of bobbin-lace
in Cumberland, far from any district where it is extensively
made, are able to sell a wide edging of coarse work, made at
the rate of one yard in 8 or 9 hours, for 6*s*. 6*d*. a yard, to
tourists and other visitors. This represents a rate of 6¾*d*. an
hour, including the cost of the cotton. These two makers,
a mother and daughter, also do hand-weaving, spinning, and
embroidery, so the amount of lace which they make is not
large and it is not likely that there would be a sale for any
considerable quantity at this relatively high price. But
there are numbers of handicraft workers in this district and
many visitors buy their work as a novelty, probably with
little regard to the price.

In Coggeshall one of the younger workers said that she
could earn 3*s*. in a working day of seven hours, but out of
this she would have to provide the material, the net on
which the lace is worked being quite expensive. The children
who used to work in the lace-rooms were paid 1*d*. a week at
first, and might receive 6*d*. a week after three years if they
were quick and industrious, while, after a further two years,
the girl of thirteen would be earning the handsome sum of
3*s*. 6*d*. weekly for full-time work. Married women who
worked at home might make 6*s*. or 7*s*. a week, or, at the
most 10*s*. a week, spending at the tambour frame every
minute available from their housework.

In the Midlands the prices paid fifty years ago are generally
described as quite good, but later they dropped until lace
was no longer worth making. Within the last ten years or
so they have increased considerably, although there has
been a slight reduction since the war, balanced by the fall
in the cost of the material.

Undoubtedly the Associations have helped to raise the standard of payment, but the workers themselves are entirely unorganized and powerless to effect any change. They are not included as members or represented in the Associations, nor are they really consulted as to the rates of payment, system of teaching, or other controversial points.

The payment is still very small for such skilled and delicate work, or, indeed, for any work at all, but the explanation always given is that there would be no sale for lace if more was paid for the making of it and if it had, consequently, to be sold at higher prices. It is difficult to give any exact statement of the relation of the sum paid to the workers to the selling-price of the lace, because the varieties of lace and of patterns are so numerous, and because the value of every piece must be estimated by the buyer on its own merits and according to the demand. Only an expert can judge of the time taken to make any particular piece, and, again, the capacities of the workers vary greatly.

There is a certain amount of foreign competition in the industry, missionaries having introduced the making of Bedfordshire lace, from the actual patterns in use in the Midlands, into the Mission schools of India and China. Owing to the low standard of living in these countries, this foreign lace, which is sold by some London shops, can be produced much more cheaply than English.

Quantities of lace are also imported from France, Belgium, and other European countries, and include some of the varieties from which the English 'Bedford' and 'Buckingham' laces were originally derived. The low cost at which this foreign lace seems to be produced operates to keep down the prices paid for English lace, particularly as very little has been done in the English industry in the way of producing new designs which, breaking away from the tradition of the French and Belgian patterns, might command a better price by virtue of originality.

vi. *Prospects.*

It is urged in favour of the encouragement of the lace industry that it is carried on by women who are physically unfitted for other work and that it never replaces any other remunerative occupation. This is generally true. There are some girls and young women who have learnt the craft recently in the classes organized by one or other of the Associations and who still do the work, but they are very

few in number. The lace-makers include girls and women
who are invalids or too delicate to go out to work, cripples,
or occasionally a girl living at home who is occupied with
field work throughout the summer and autumn and makes
lace during the winter and spring. Girls temporarily at home
for a few months between situations also make lace, but
elderly women, especially widows, many of them old age
pensioners and the occupants of almshouses, constitute the
bulk of lace-makers.

Lace-making is in many ways very suitable for a part-
time occupation for cottage women. The pillow and bobbins,
once obtained, will last a lifetime and the cost of the thread
is small. The pillow does not take up very much room,
the work can be taken up or left at almost any moment,
and, even if the worker's hands are not overclean, the lace
will not be soiled as her hands only touch the bobbins and
pins, except when she comes to the end of the ' down ' and
has to roll up the piece of lace and ' set up ' again. Undoubtedly the weekly 3s. to 7s. earned by many old women is
a precious addition to their incomes, and in one district it
was stated that the recent fall in farm-labourers' wages had
caused many women to fetch out the lace pillow which had
been put aside for many years.

Although the workers generally say that they enjoy the
work, yet no one was found making lace for her own pleasure
or her own use. Lace-makers generally appeared, to judge
from their surroundings, to be the poorest inhabitants of
the village.

Many people with the most excellent intentions, are
working hard to encourage and develop the industry. They
feel that such a beautiful craft should not be allowed to
die out.

The evidence obtainable in the Midlands does not indicate
any really widespread demand for lace classes amongst
village girls and women. In some villages demonstrations
have been arranged by the Women's Institutes, which,
including, as they do, women of all ages, should be able to
discover whether any are keen to learn the craft. But the
almost invariable result of the demonstrations is that little
interest is taken, except by one or two old lace-makers, who
like to compare the teacher's methods and patterns with
their own. Some other women like to watch the work, but
few show any desire to learn it. The fact that the initial
stages of learning are so slow, that it takes so long to complete
a piece of work, and that pillows are bulky to carry about,

are all difficulties when the craft is considered in the light of Women's Institute work.

It would be regrettable if the craft of lace-making were to be entirely lost, but could not those people who are working to save it from extinction apply their efforts more wisely to the teaching of this craft to girls who can better afford to spend so much labour on making beautiful things for their own use ?   Of one hundred village girls of the working class who are taught to make pillow lace, it is doubtful whether ten will make a yard of lace for their own use after they cease to attend the classes, whereas, if they had been taught to embroider in simple stitches, such as darning and cross-stitch, it is probable that at least half of them would practise this craft to a considerable extent for the adornment of their own clothing.   Lace-making is either a sweated industry, practised only by the most needy, or a delightful hobby for leisured people whose time is not reckoned in terms of the necessities of life.

CHAPTER IV

HOME CRAFTS AND INDUSTRIES

i. *Distribution and Organization.*

THE workers in what are classified as ' home crafts and industries ' are to a great extent isolated individuals or small local groups of crafts -men and -women. Their classification under this heading has been explained.[1] There are numerous guilds and societies for the promotion of handicrafts and home industries and for the sale of their work, and a great many of the scattered workers belong to one or other of these organizations. Sometimes they are local, including a group of people in a certain district, while in other cases the members are widely scattered, their connecting link being a common aim or the practice of one common craft. Often a shop or agency is carried on by such societies, others only hold exhibitions from time to time. The various associations for helping lace-makers described in the preceding chapter do not, for the most part, have any connexion with other handicraft workers, although some of them are also concerned with embroidery.

One of the most important and oldest of these organizations is the Home Arts and Industries Association, which was founded in 1884, with the main object of reviving and developing crafts which were in danger of dying out. At first these were stimulated only as home industries and as classes for the sake of recreation, character training, and the decoration of the workers' homes. But soon a need was felt for some further outlet for the work produced, and so the annual exhibition held in London was inaugurated. The Association also undertook the training of teachers in its early days, but later this became unnecessary owing to the number of classes in craft work organized by Art Schools and by various bodies. The work of the Association is now chiefly to advise and to assist in the formation of handicraft classes, which often develop into industries, and to organize, for the sale of the work, the annual exhibitions. In addition, there has recently been opened a permanent depot attached to the London offices, where work is on sale throughout the

[1] See Chapter I, p. 4.

year. Sales are good, and during the summer a number of American visitors are attracted to this showroom by means of judicious advertisement through hotels and clubs.

The Home Arts and Industries Association includes isolated workers, affiliated societies and industries—both 'developed industries' (those which are self-supporting, with full-time workers and paid management) and 'partially developed industries' (those which are only partially self-supporting, with voluntary help in management). Members pay an annual subscription, but the Association is not self-supporting and has to appeal for donations to its funds. Its influence in the matter of standard in craftsmanship is a valuable one, all work sent to the exhibitions being judged by experts and required to pass a certain standard before it is accepted for sale. A commission of 10 per cent. on sales is charged. A few wholesale orders are received through the Association from the ordinary trade and it has been found that some of the work can be sold satisfactorily in this way, although the small country industries of the type usually affiliated to the Association are not as a rule adapted to the production of work in wholesale quantities.

The number of individual handicraft workers seems to be greatly on the increase at the present time and the Association is constantly receiving new applications from them for affiliation. The well-known Ruskin Pottery, which can no longer be classed among these amateur enterprises, is an outstanding example of the growth of a flourishing industry from a very small beginning, in this case with only two or three workers. This is one of the few affiliated industries which is easily able to produce goods in wholesale quantities and it now supplies a very extensive market.

Amongst the numerous other organizations of craft workers a few, fairly representative of the chief types, may be mentioned. The Dorset Arts and Crafts Society is interested in the development of village industries in that county ; the Northumberland Handicrafts Guild holds classes in Embroidery, Wood-carving, and Basket-making, and organizes exhibitions ; the Artificers' Guild comprises a group of craftsmen living in different places, metal-workers, potters, and others, and under its auspices the weaving studio in which mentally deficient people are employed, is carried on. The Guild has a shop in London and another in Cambridge, and is notable for the very high standard of all the work sold there. These craftsmen are really specialists of a high order who give their whole time to their crafts.

The Knox Guild of Design and Craft, which was founded in 1912, stands for ' simplicity and sincerity in design and craftsmanship '. Advice relative to starting design and craft work for ' the joy of the working ' is given by the Guild, which includes among its members workers in leather, in metal and in horn, needleworkers, raffia workers, weavers, dyers, and spinners. The Dorset blacksmith, mentioned elsewhere, who designs and makes fire-tongs, latches, door-knockers, and other decorative work, is a member of the Guild, and, together with other members, has shown some excellent work at the exhibitions which are arranged through it.

The well-known Chipping Campden group of craftsmen is one of the oldest of the modern ' Guilds ', and still of considerable importance and interest, in spite of the collapse of the original organization. It was started in London about thirty-five years ago as the ' Guild of Handicrafts ', in connexion with Toynbee Hall, and later became a limited company. About fifteen or twenty years ago the group of workers moved to Chipping Campden, a delightful but decaying old town on the fringe of the Cotswolds. The whole colony, including the wives and families of the craftsmen, numbered about seventy persons, and Campden was chosen as a centre because, having declined from its old position as one of the most important centres of the wool trade to that of a quiet and isolated country town, it contained a number of empty houses, whilst a deserted silk-mill near by, a relic of a later, but already extinct, industrial activity, could be utilized for workrooms. About half a dozen years after the move to Campden the Guild went into liquidation, the cause of its failure being, apparently, the one common to so many well-intentioned efforts—a lack of business ability. When the Guild broke up, however, many individual workers remained, and wrought iron-work, sculpture and wood-carving, silver-smithing, building, and cabinet-making are still carried on in Campden by former members of the Guild, whilst two craftsmen who have joined the group more recently do book-binding and make stained glass. The group now seems to be organized on lines far more practical than in the beginning, but their great difficulty is that of distribution. A shop in Bond Street which the Guild carried on for some years proved to be too expensive. A small shop was at one time kept in Campden itself, and the very beautiful enamel work which used to be, but is no longer made there, was sold successfully. But many of the things now produced are not suitable for exhibition in a shop, and the big pieces of sculpture and wood-carving, often made for churches, must, for the most part, be done to special orders. Campden is not on any main road, few trains stop at the small station, and although it is only a dozen miles south of Stratford-on-Avon and in the midst of the tourist-haunted Cotswold country, it attracts fewer visitors than its near neighbour, Broadway, which lies on a main road. Thus, the Chipping Campden craftsmen feel to some extent the need for a closer contact with some market beyond their own immediate locality.

The guilds and societies described above give some idea of the many different organizations which exist for the encouragement of handicraft work. Of a different kind is the work of the Women's Institutes. The teaching of handicrafts forms a part of the broadly planned educational work which is carried on through this organization. The primary aim, as far as handicraft work is concerned, is to awaken and to keep alive the interest of countrywomen both in ancient home industries and in modern craftsmanship, and to provide them with opportunities for learning crafts which can be applied to the beautifying of their own homes and which are of value to them as recreation and change from their usual household duties. Thus the Institutes play a useful part in the general revival of craftsmanship, for the principle is upheld that anything which is worth making is worth the maker's utmost care and trouble, and only the best work of which she is capable is good enough for even the simplest thing. A Guild of Learners, comprising both those who are willing to perfect themselves and those skilled workers who have already passed tests both in workmanship and in ability to impart their knowledge to others, encourages the workers to attain to and not to fall back from a high standard. Demonstrations of different crafts are given at Institute meetings, and if the members' interest is thus aroused classes in some particular craft follow. Handicraft schools are arranged by head-quarters for the training of teachers, and the work of any members who are willing to pass a test and teach others is judged by experts in each craft. Exhibitions are held both by individual Institutes and by the County Federations, Women's Institute stalls are arranged at local agricultural or other shows, whilst the National Federation organizes a biennial exhibition including work from all parts of England and Wales.

The amount of handicraft work done by different Institutes

or counties varies considerably. It depends on the character
of the country people of any particular district, on their
opportunities, and also, to a great extent, on the local leaders
of the movement. In some cases so much interest has been
aroused and such a quantity of work has been produced that
the need for some outlet has arisen and shops for the sale
of work have been opened. In any case, a good many things
made by the members are generally sold at shows and sales
arranged by the Institutes for the sake of raising funds for
their own organization. The National Federation is in no
sense a trading organization, and any sales must be arranged
by the separate Institutes or by the County Federations. The
Dorset Federation of Women's Institutes co-operates with
the Dorset Arts and Crafts Society to hold joint exhibitions with them, and organizes some of the women's home
industries which are found in many villages of this county.

There are certain groups of handicraft workers who
represent a survival of some ancient indigenous industry.
The cutting of rushes and sedge and the weaving of them
into baskets, mats, and plait to be used for various purposes,
is still a regular industry, chiefly carried out by men, in
a few districts of England, notably in Norfolk and at certain
places on the Bedford Ouse and the Nene.[1] In certain cases
this craft has been taken up by women, either individual
workers or members of Women's Institutes, who carry it
out on rather different lines. Thus, at Wimborne and
Blandford, in Dorset, a part-time home industry for women
has been developed for making up into mats, baskets,
hassocks and other things the rushes which were formerly
woven here into workmen's baskets or used for the seats of
chairs and by coopers. The work is now organized through
the Women's Institutes in co-operation with the Dorset Arts
and Crafts Society. In Hampshire also, the Institute
members make up rushes and sedge into hats, mats, and
baskets. In Hunts. the Women's Institutes have not only
done some very good rush-work but have also organized
with some success the cutting, drying, and storing of rushes
for sale to individual workers. It is doubtful whether they
can supply to any workers beyond the radius of their own
County Federation at a price more advantageous than that
charged by the ordinary dealer, although they have had
orders from workers as far distant as Scotland. In this
county the ordinary rush-working industry has long been

---

[1] See vol. ii, *Osier Growing, Basketry Industries and Some Rural Factories*,
Part I, Chapter III, ' Rush, Sedge, and Reed Industries '.

extinct, although it is still carried on in the neighbouring counties, but an old rush-cutter, who supplies the rushes to coopers, still carries on his business near St. Ives. In Northamptonshire the Institutes have also taken up rush-work, and at King's Sutton, on the Cherwell, south of Banbury, rushes are cut locally for the use of the Institute. In Norfolk, where the plaiting of rush and sedge horse-collars is still done by many of the marshmen, rush-work has been practised by the Women's Institutes, but there are only very few women who do much of it, one of whom at one time made her living by the industry. She learnt from one of the old collar-makers and combines their traditional skill with originality of design. The Institutes in Suffolk are making an attempt to use the small three-cornered rushes, which grow in ditches, for decorative work, these being more easily gathered than the larger ones, which grow in deep water, and, as they have no pith, drying more quickly. They do not seem to be utilized in any of the older rush industries, possibly because they are small and are not found in great quantities, so that the labour of collecting enough of them for any considerable amount of work would be too great, but they seem to be particularly suitable for a women's home craft and for weaving into small articles, and so the venture may meet with success.

An industry which is somewhat akin to rush-work is straw-plaiting. This also still survives in its old form in certain Hertfordshire villages,[1] but as out-work done for large factories and never as an independent industry. In Essex, however, where no straw-plaiting out-work is now done, one of the old workers turns her traditional skill to account in making baskets, hats, and other things, which she sells through the exhibitions held by the Women's Institute. She lives between Saffron Walden and Halstead, which were the centres of the straw-plaiting industry of Essex. In the museum at the former place there is exhibited a basket and a cradle made of straw-plait by one of the old workers. Although the craft of straw-plaiting is adaptable to the making not only of hats but also of any varieties of light basket-work, whilst the material is cheap and easily obtainable from a friendly farmer, and there must be many of the former workers still alive who are skilled in plaiting both whole and split straws in a great number of designs, yet such attempts as have been made to revive this industry

[1] See vol. ii, *Osier Growing, Basketry Industries and Some Rural Factories*, Part II, Chapter III, ' Outwork for Factories '.

more extensively as a home craft for women do not seem to have met with success.

The quilting which is done by many countrywomen in Northumberland and in the village of Wykeham in Yorkshire is a very old craft which is now being encouraged through the Women's Institutes. Traditional patterns are still in use, some of them of great antiquity.

In a Sussex town an industry, which has now grown beyond the dimensions of a home craft, has been developed in an interesting way from the skill of an old countryman. This man used to make rough caps called ' battlejacks ' of rabbit skins, of two designs known as ' four-pointed ' and ' six-pointed '. About thirty years ago a saddler's journey-man copied one of these to make a cap for himself, and then, realizing the possibilities of the craft, joined forces with the saddler and others to start an industry. The original idea was to employ women as home-workers, but a few years ago the industry was developed on different lines, by new pro-moters. A certain amount of newspaper publicity was obtained and the interesting origin of the industry was exploited to the full. The design has been registered and the demand for leather caps for motoring has given the industry such excellent chances of extension that it is now carried on on factory, rather than village, industry lines.

Suffolk labourers were expert, at one time, at making straw mats to be used as door-mats or on the floors of carts. There are one or two men who still possess this skill, and mats of this kind have been made for the Women's Institute hut in a village near Ipswich. No further attempt seems to have been made to keep this craft alive, but the making of mats from sail-cloth and manilla twine, which is another old Suffolk industry, is still said to be a spare-time occupation for fishermen.

It is also in Suffolk that the gypsies make lanterns out of bottles. This is a very elementary kind of handicraft, if indeed it can be so called, but it demands just the qualities in which gypsies excel, namely, ingenuity in utilizing other-wise worthless materials, and deftness of fingers. The neck is knocked off the bottle, which is fitted into a tin frame-work with a handle, and the lantern is complete. A handi-craft shop in Walberswick retails them at 2s. 6d., and is probably able to obtain this inflated price because of their quaintness.

Gypsies have a knowledge of many queer crafts, which, from the fact that each one usually survives amongst them only in some particular district, would seem to be relics of traditional native work and not of gypsy origin. Miss Woods describes a certain type of basket which they make in the Oxford district.[1] In Sussex, also, they make split hazel baskets and clothes pegs. In Essex they used to extract the white cylindrical pith in long, flexible pieces from the small field rushes, which was then made up into little fancy baskets. These were very fragile and of no use whatever, but trippers would buy them for a few pence because of their novelty and prettiness. Gypsies do not excel in craftsmanship, but their ingenuity in the use of the simple materials to hand, and of improvised tools, might provide ideas for the home craftsman.

Amongst other home industries recently revived or developed which have some direct link with ancient crafts of the district may be mentioned the smocking industry carried on by a Sussex Women's Institute, in which this very beautiful old work is applied to the decoration of garments for modern wear. The knitting industry of the Yorkshire Dales, which was widely known and extensively carried on until late in the nineteenth century, and which relied originally on the wool locally grown, carded and spun, is recalled by the many women in the colliery towns of the north who earn sometimes their whole livelihood by knitting, on treadle machines, thick, warm socks for the miners. In agricultural districts this work has lately been taken up by a number of women, who get plenty of orders from farmhands, and who have been enabled, through the Women's Institute organization, to buy knitting-machines on easy terms. In this case, however, the newer industry has no real connexion with the old one, although its lingering tradition may have suggested the craft of knitting to the organizers.

In addition to these home industries or groups of handicraft workers who have a direct link with ancient industries, there are many others, promoted by the Women's Institutes or by other organizations, or carried on by individual workers, which have been recently developed on no such traditional basis. Where there is a good local market for handiwork amongst people who are particularly appreciative of beauty in any form, there is likely to be more of this work done than in places where the main interest of the population lies in machine processes and industrial life and where any kind of handicraft is often stigmatized as mere waste of time. The villages and small country towns of the South

[1] See *The Rural Industries round Oxford.*

of England have a number of depots for the sale of all kinds of hand-made things, for example, at Haslemere, Petersfield, Limpsfield, Sevenoaks, Canterbury, and in the neighbour-hood of Guildford, and of Sandwich. There are many individual workers in all kinds of crafts. Besides the Battle-jack industry mentioned above, a novel industry is that of collecting poultry feathers and making them up into feather brooms and trimmings. At Petersfield there is a group of workers whose activities include not only hand-made jewellery, book-binding, picture framing, embroidery, and dressmaking, stained and painted wood and decorative building work, but also the sale of new and second-hand books, and a tea shop is also carried on. A settlement of this kind, in a town such as Petersfield, picturesque and of antiquarian interest, has all the elements which are likely to endow a craft-working enterprise with success.

A small industry in which three or four disabled ex-service men are employed, at Wadhurst, turns out stools with simple oak frames, well made and put together with wooden pegs, and seated with twisted sea-grass. The coiled strands of grass, stretched across the seat from side to side and from front to back, but not woven or plaited together, make a seat of novel and attractive appearance and of considerable comfort. Another small home industry in the south-eastern counties, which probably owes much of its success to the originality of its products, is the painting of wooden bowls. The bowls are obtained from the turner of Bucklebury Common, in Berkshire,[1] and effective designs of flowers and fruit are painted on the unstained wood in colours which will bear wiping with a damp cloth for cleaning. Thus the bowls are suitable for holding fruit and look well with the simple furniture of unstained and unpolished elm or oak, the making of which is now being undertaken by a few small rural firms.[2]

The Lake District is another locality remarkable for the large amount of artistic enterprise to be found there. As well as the weavers (see Chapter II), many of whom also embroider and make lace, there is a small pottery; and other workers, most of them in connexion with the Women's Institutes, make rugs, fur gloves, children's clothing, and bags of leather and of straw. The Institutes take advantage of the presence of so many skilled craftsmen by organizing

---

[1] See K. S. Woods, *The Rural Industries round Oxford*.
[2] See vol. i, *Timber and Underwood Industries and Some Village Work-shops*.

classes in various kinds of work. Apart from the making
of things for sale, there are a great many countrywomen who
make rugs for their own homes, this craft being very widely
practised in this district. There are also two metal-working
industries, organized on the principle of winter work for
summer sale, one of which, at Keswick, has been carried
on for thirty years and has earned a wide reputation.

There are no notable handicraft activities in the other
northern counties, excepting Yorkshire. Here an outstanding point is the artificial flower making carried on by a
Women's Institute in a village near Northallerton. The
flowers are made of scraps of silk and other materials and
are designed chiefly for the trimming of hats. The workmanship is delicate and there might be a good sale for the
flowers, although it has not yet been extensively developed.
Many other handicrafts are practised by members of Women's
Institutes in other Yorkshire villages, glove-making being
the most popular and, in many respects, the most successful,
but, as is generally the case, it is only a very small proportion
of the members attending the classes who ever keep up their
enthusiasm sufficiently to produce more than one or two
pairs after the classes are over. The Women's Institute
organization is, however, still very young in Yorkshire.
Other leather-work is done, net-making has been taken up,
and there is considerable interest also in hand-loom weaving,
several workers having been helped, through the organization,
to obtain looms and other apparatus.

Amongst other counties Dorset is one of the most notable
for handicraft work, perhaps owing to the existence here
of the active Dorset Arts and Crafts Society, which co-operates with the County Federation of Women's Institutes.
The Blandford Rush Industry, already mentioned (page 76),
flourishes, in spite of Dutch competition in all kinds of
rush-work, which has caused the decay of old rush industries
in other parts of England. A button industry at Lytchett
Minster, soft toy making at Monkton, the Bloxworth sunbonnet industry, started for crippled women or those otherwise incapacitated for ordinary work, and the Studland Arts
and Crafts, which combines an artist's individual work with
training for students in leather work, ornamental wood-work,
and embroidery, are examples of home industries in villages
which provide a number of women with part-time work.
The sunbonnet industry, which also produces frocks, overalls
and jumpers, was founded in 1913, and although when
visited in 1921 it had dwindled considerably, there was still

a good sale for the work, and Women's Institutes in other counties had been encouraged by this success, in work which is easily learnt and not difficult to start, to organize similar industries. A filet-lace class at Rushmore, affiliated to the Home Arts and Industries Association, has produced excellent work, but, as in the Midlands and Honiton lace industries (see Chapter III), the competition of machine-made goods, the best of which are of considerable beauty and durability, may make it difficult for the makers of lace by hand to earn enough to keep the industry on its feet. In this craft it is probable that the older and wider-reaching organizations for promoting lace-making in the Midlands have a good command of the limited market that exists for hand-made lace, so that small new village industries have little chance of success, although filet-lace, being a new departure, might find an outlet, especially if combined with embroidery and needlework industries, so that it could be sold on made-up garments.

In the adjoining county of Wiltshire the Longleat shoe industry was started during the war to meet the difficulty of obtaining cheap house-shoes. Fortnightly classes were held at Frome and Warminster and in two neighbouring villages, and work was taken home to be completed. Although the industry was very successful during the war, the sales fell off later when other inexpensive shoes came again upon the market. From this centre instruction was given to several Women's Institutes, and slipper-making became a popular home industry amongst the women. It is probable that it will continue to be practised to meet home needs, although it may not be possible to sell much of the work. An embroidery industry, started thirty years ago at Fisherton-de-la-Mere, now employs a number of workers in other counties as well as in this neighbourhood. The object of the promoters was to give occupation to disabled persons of either sex, and to revive old embroideries on hand-made linen. Owing to the beauty of design and the excellent workmanship which is characteristic of the products of this industry, there is a good sale for the work, mainly through the medium of exhibitions.

The handicraft work of the Women's Institutes of Warwickshire provides a good example of the successful development of home industries, through the enthusiasm, ability and patient endeavours of the promotors, in a county where there are few survivals of the older village crafts, owing, probably, to the fatal influence of the surrounding industrial districts, but in which there are particularly good opportunities for the sale of work to the tourists who throng such towns as Warwick and Stratford-on-Avon. The county also seems to be fortunate in possessing a large proportion of people who can give time to the organization of home industries and who help to provide a market. Two shops are carried on by the Women's Institutes and the things made for sale include gloves, baskets, raffia-work, rush mats, soft toys, needlework and embroidery, knitted and crochet goods, and bottled fruit. Most of these are the output of village women, each of whom produces only a very small amount in her spare time. There are, however, two makers of cane baskets who have taken up craft-work as a supplementary or sole means of livelihood, one of whom employs two or three village girls as helpers. Cane dyed in bright colours to make decorative baskets of original design and shape is used, and the industry seems to contain considerable promise of further development. One of these workers has also taken up the dyeing of cane and raffia for sale to other handicraft workers, in which she is meeting with success. Gloves are the chief output of the ordinary Women's Institute workers of this county, and one small group of Institutes has gained quite a wide reputation for the excellence of its products in this line, and executes many orders received by post from customers who have seen the work at exhibitions.

Amongst other groups of handicraft workers mention should be made of the St. Ives Handicraft Guild, where, in addition to weaving, some beautiful raffia-work is done. At Woodbridge, in Suffolk, there is a small glove and mocassin industry, employing several girls in a workroom. There is a shop for the sale of the goods.

A small home industry which may be found in many countries and which is dependent on one of the occupations subsidiary to agriculture, is the preparation of moleskins. The skins are dried and sold to furriers, and this forms a lucrative side-line to the business of mole-catching, which, in itself, is generally carried on as a part-time industry. supplementary to summer work on the land. The sale of the moleskins brings in more than the fee for mole-catching. Such is the value of the moleskins, in fact, especially in the best season, from the beginning of December until the end of January, that the mole-catcher will often work on land for which he is paid no fee. The skins are only saleable from November until the end of April, and therefore the moles are only trapped at that time. During a few weeks of the winter season the mole-catcher may, if the weather is favourable, obtain skins to the value of £5 or £6 weekly. The usual custom is for the man or his wife merely to dry the skins by pinning them out on a board, and to sell them thus to the furrier, but many women, having learnt the craft of skin-curing through the classes held by the Women's Institutes, have carried out the whole process of dressing the skins, and it is possible that there is an opening for further development of this work as a home industry for the winter months, moleskin now being of considerable value as a fur.

In Herefordshire a fur-craft industry has grown up in con-nexion with a rabbitry started during the war with the object of increasing the food supply. There is room for 400 rabbits and, now that meat is not such an important object, the rabbits are bred mainly for their fur, and the skins are dressed and made up into many articles. There are, however, no organized sales of handicraft work in this county, and the craft is carried on mainly as a hobby, except for the production of work for the Institute exhibitions. Some Norfolk Institute members also breed rabbits and cure the skins. In many other counties fur-craft is taken up by Women's Institute members, but there is often considerable difficulty experienced in obtaining skins, because rabbits, either wild or specially bred, are usually sold direct to the town poulterers, who, in turn, sell the skins to wholesale dealers.

Women's Institutes in other counties have taken up handicraft work for sale, sometimes on a very small scale, with little or no central organization, the separate workers disposing of their output each by her own efforts. In other cases there is some organized method of sale, and sometimes a shop window or stall in connexion with the county office is gradually developed into an independent shop. The county office may thus provide Institute craftswomen with a very useful opportunity of showing their work and making it known whilst they test the market, without undertaking the risk and expense of opening a shop until the way has thus been prepared. In Northamptonshire special attention is paid to needlework by the Institute organization, with the idea of replacing to some extent the out-work in button-holing and in finishing shirts and pinafores, which was formerly given out to many countrywomen from numerous factories in the county which now have machinery for doing this work on the premises. In Cambridgeshire the organiza-tion has served a useful purpose in putting village workers, needle-women and knitters in touch with private customers in Cambridge and elsewhere. Lincolnshire is one of the counties in which very little interest is taken in handicraft work. In the Lindsey and Kesteven divisions Institutes are numerous, but in Holland and the Isle of Axholme districts hardly any have come into being, owing, perhaps, to the scarcity of leisured folk who would be able to give their time to the organization, and also to the fact that in these districts the women are so fully occupied by their work on the land during the greater part of the year that they would be inclined to say that they had no time for Institute meetings. In the Isle of Ely, however, where similar conditions prevail, the Institute movement has spread, although it is found that, owing to the amount of manual labour which the women perform in the fields, the more intellectual recreations and activities of the Institutes appeal to them rather than craft-work. When the difficulties have been overcome and Institutes formed, as is already beginning to happen in Holland, these women, with their sense of independence and enterprise, should prove able to carry on in a truly demo-cratic and vivacious manner, although it is probable that lectures, study circles, and music will be demanded by the majority of members rather than work for their hands.

In the Kesteven and Lindsey divisions of Lincolnshire it was often stated that the women were not interested in handicrafts and would never take up anything with the perseverance necessary to found a successful home industry. But in the course of visits to more than a dozen Institutes, mentioned by the organizers as those in which handicraft work had been most energetically taken up, it was not found that in any case had an attempt been made to organize such an industry. The usual plan seems to be for a new course of instruction in some other craft to be arranged for as soon as the members are fairly proficient in one. The greater number of these Institutes were in villages of only a few hundred inhabitants and obviously, if a village industry is to be organized in such a place, some market beyond the village must be found. Very little has been attempted in this direction. The secretary of a Women's Institute near Grantham had approached the shops in that town to try to get orders for hand-sewn gloves, but the price offered was so low (5s. 6d. a pair) that nothing further resulted. It is often said that the village women are too poor to afford the initial outlay on materials, and little advantage seems to have been taken of the existing organization, which would make a scheme for co-operative buying easy to arrange. There are a few individual handicraft workers in Lincolnshire, including a spinner for the Sussex weavers and two glove-makers. A hand-loom weaver has a few girls from the village working for her, but, except for this one case, the women of the farm-workers' families in this county have not taken up handicraft work, either for sale or even for their own use, to any great extent. Yet the county is one in which the villages are small and isolated, and, apart from the Women's Institutes, there is a marked lack of any organizations for providing education, recreation, or stimulating co-operative enterprise. It is therefore probable that home industries in the villages would supply a much needed source of interest and of remuneration, and the absence of them is probably due, not really to any lack of ability on the part of Lincolnshire women, but to the lack of the skilled enthusiasts to whose individual efforts nearly all successful village industries in other counties owe their foundation and often, in the earlier years of their existence at least, their very life. The very conditions of isolation and stagnation which would make a handicraft industry so valuable also constitute the greatest difficulties in the way of founding one, and it is quite true that an enterprise of this sort can only be carried on successfully by willing workers who desire it and believe in its efficiency. But it is hard for a country woman with the merest smattering of education, who has never been brought into contact with any one but her neighbours in her own and the few nearest villages, to believe that she herself can, after a little teaching and some steady and patient practice, experience the artist's joy in creation and, moreover, find customers for her handiwork, and earn a little precious income of her own. Demonstrations in simple crafts, exhibitions of the work of other village women, and well organized methods of sale, might convince her of all this, and it would then be found that she is as well able as her sister in Warwickshire or elsewhere to carry on a home industry which would provide her with both pleasure and profit.

The position in Lincolnshire, as regards the Women's Institutes and the existence of home industries, has been examined at considerable length because it illustrates the point that the non-existence of such industries in any district does not necessarily imply that the women of the district have no need or inclination to carry one on. Often it is only the result of a lack of individual enterprise in this particular direction. It is true, however, that Lincolnshire is curiously lacking in the craftsmen of the ordinary village industries. A great deal of sheep-netting is made and a certain amount of rope. In the wood industries the only notable skilled craftsmen, apart from the usual carpenters, are the ' rivers ', who split ash-poles for fencing. Basket-making is not extensively carried on, except by a very large firm in Grantham which hardly falls within the category of rural industries. These are almost the only modern crafts of any importance which are to be found in the county, neither is there any tradition of ancient craftsmanship which could be compared to the linen industry of the Lake District, the still surviving lace-making of Bedfordshire and Bucks, or the Coventry ribbon-weaving.

It is possible that where an old industry, such as lace-making or straw-plaiting, has been extensively carried on in the villages of a certain district until recent times, the country women have inherited a certain traditional skill in and knowledge of hand-work which would serve as a good foundation for a new or revived village industry. Lace-making has not been extensively taken up by the Women's Institutes, probably because there are already so many organizations for the development of it. The desirability of artificially stimulating this industry is doubtful, because of the danger of encouraging the employment of sweated labour. But if village women would make for their own use the really beautiful lace, the patterns for which are in the possession of many of them, then the encouragement of the craft and the further development of it would be an excellent object, and one which the Women's Institute organization is fitted to achieve. It is probable, however, that, owing to the great amount of time which must be devoted to the work, lace-making is a craft which is doomed to extinction as far as working women are concerned.

An aspect of the work of the Women's Institutes in many counties which comes up for criticism is that often the nature of handicraft work is not related to particular local circumstances, such as the survival of skill, traditional knowledge in a craft which may be nearly extinct as an industry, and local supplies of raw material. In taking up basketry work and making willow baskets of the ordinary local types, the workers perhaps consider too little the precarious condition of the regular basket-making industry. On the other hand, those Institutes which have taken up rush-work, employing a local rush-cutter or even harvesting the rushes for themselves, are making excellent use of local raw material to hand. The Institutes in the counties of Hertford and Bedford seem only to have explored in the straw-plaiting industry the chances of reviving this industry in order to supply factories, for which object the craft is nearly extinct. Yet it is probable that many of the old straw-plaiters could, through the medium of Institute classes, impart their knowledge to others, and straw-plait could successfully be utilized for decorative purposes, in somewhat the same way as rush-plait and raffia.

There are many work-rooms for disabled ex-service men, toy-making being a favourite craft with them. There are also a number of individual workers of this kind, some of whom find that wooden figures, cut out with a fret-saw and painted, command a good sale, particularly if the maker has some capacity for original design. From the Enham Village Centre, near Bournemouth, come many kinds of wood-work, coat-hangers decorated with a figure or head cut out of the wood being one of the latest and very successful products of these work-rooms. Raffia and cane basketry forms a large part of the output of the ex-service handicraft workers, some good work coming from a Norwich centre, whilst at a Colchester work-shop some attractive jewellery is made in good designs of an unusual character.

The metal-working industries are of a somewhat different type from the other handicraft work mentioned in this chapter, in that they are not to any great extent home industries, being more suitable to organization in work-shops. Most of them have originated as classes organized to provide a hobby for lads and men of the working class in the winter evenings. One of these industries, which has been carried on in a Cambridgeshire village for thirty years, is a good example of the method of organization. This particular enterprise has for some time been subsidized by the County Council, but in some other cases these classes are carried on independently. As a rule the output of a class receiving a County Council grant may not be sold, lest other industries of the same nature run on ordinary commercial lines should complain. But since the persons doing this metal work are farm labourers who are not ordinarily engaged in a craft requiring such manual skill as is here needed, and who only carry on this work for a few hours weekly, they are not likely to acquire the speed and skill of a regular craftsman. The industry is organized and carried on by the founder and seems to depend on him for its existence. He is responsible for the selling of the work, choosing of designs and, generally, provides the stimulus. Two work-rooms and a show-room are rented. The repoussé work could be done at home, but the comradeship and the comparison of the work, and the friendly rivalry which result, are an important element in the whole enterprise. The workers are any village lads and men who care to come, of ages varying from 14 to 40. There are also two men employed regularly, this being necessary to ensure the proper execution of any orders which may be received. Several different master-craftsmen have given instruction, but one of the regular employees is now sufficiently skilled to teach the others. The voluntary workers attend on three evenings a week from October to April and work from about seven to eight-thirty. Each man pays 2s. on joining the class and in return for this receives the two most necessary tools. Other tools are the property of the organizer and are borrowed as required. Each article made by the men is, on completion, transferred to the show-room and account is kept of every piece of work. From time to time stock is taken in the show-room and each man is paid for as much of his work as has been sold; 20 per cent. of the price of the article goes towards running expenses and the remainder to the workers. The amount earned by the men, if all their work is sold, averages about 6d. an evening, i.e. about 4d. an hour. They attend as much for the interest in the work as for the sake of the earnings. Only work which passes a certain standard is taken into the show-room for sale and a man generally attends the classes for about three months before he attains this proficiency. The greatest difficulty experienced by the organizer is to teach the men to work carefully.

The craftsmanship of this class varies a great deal, the repoussé work being more commonplace and sometimes showing signs of carelessness, while much of the hammered copper and silver is excellent. The design of some of the things is evolved by the workers. Probably the men with most aptitude are more attracted by this work, which is more skilled and gives the craftsman more scope for originality. On the whole, considering that the men have so little opportunity for acquiring skill, the standard of the output is remarkable.

The classes in beaten brass and copper work at Heversham and Keswick in the Lake District have also been carried on for thirty years. At Keswick, where the organization is on a large scale, there is a paid manager, but the smaller enterprise at Heversham is organized by a voluntary worker, a woman, who herself teaches the class. Both these classes are now established on a sound commercial basis, and it is considered in the villages a great privilege to be allowed to attend them. Sufficient profit has been made to build show-rooms for the goods. In this case the men are paid according to a fixed scale for all work done, and after supplies of material have been bought and overhead expenses paid, any further profits are divided amongst the workmen. Each worker buys material from the stock as he requires it. Some boys develop no talent for the work and give it up, but others who become proficient buy tools for themselves and take work home to do. These, however, continue to attend the class from time to time in order to keep their work up to standard and also for the sake of the company which the class provides.

There are several metal-working industries in the south-western counties. A copper-beating shop at Hayle is a regular full-time industry, and in Salisbury an ornamental iron-work industry, which was started as a class under the Home Arts and Industries Association, outgrew its original scope and was sold to a cycle shop in the town. This is now a very successful industry and more orders are received than the craftsmen can carry out. It was stated that apprentices would be taken if lads could be found who had had some experience in iron-work. In a village near Honiton some beautiful silver work is done by a man and his wife. The man has been both an employee and a designer and manufacturer in Birmingham, and, as a young student at Sheffield, came under the influence of Ruskin. He came to the south of England to start work independently because he believes that in the agricultural districts are the only possible fields for artistic development in craft-work. The Newlyn copper industry was started by two artists with a class of boys whom they taught to carry out their own designs in beaten copper work. They have never attempted to evoke designing ability in the workers themselves but have attained a good standard of execution and, by means of the Home Arts and Industries exhibitions, the work has become known in many parts of the world and there is a ready sale for all that they make. Many of their designs are registered and are therefore copyright. This is a wise precaution, for much of the value of the work of these small industries consists in the originality of the design, and in metal work particularly designs are very easily copied.

ii. *The Principal Crafts.*

Glove-making. Glove-making is one of the favourite and most successful of the crafts taken up by the Women's Institutes. It is an easy industry to start, although the necessary initial outlay in material is comparatively large, no special apparatus is required and the technique of the work is simple ; care and patience must, however, be applied. The cutting out of the gloves is the process requiring most skill, and in some Institutes this is all done by one specially expert member. In the small glove industry in Suffolk, unconnected with the Institutes, all the cutting out is done by members of the proprietor's family, the secrets of this craft having never been imparted to any outsiders, although several girls in the neighbourhood are employed to sew the gloves. The patterns in use by the Dunchurch Women's Institute industry in Warwickshire have all been designed by the organizers and perfected after many experiments. For washable and for fur-lined leather gloves as well as for the rough garden and household gloves, the skilled Institute gloveresses can get as good a fit as is necessary. The professional cutter with many years' experience and with a good stock of material can use it economically by careful selection of skins and parts of skins for particular purposes, and thus secure good wearing quality at the least cost. Individual glove-makers are sometimes hampered by lack of ready money with which to purchase a good stock of skins, and unless they can obtain several pounds' worth at once they may be forced to cut them extravagantly, especially if several orders of different kinds are to be executed. Therefore a number of glove-makers working together (as may be the case in an Institute), who can purchase the skins co-operatively and leave the cutting to one of their number, will be able to produce gloves far more economically than if purchasing individually. It has been suggested that where, as in the Yeovil district, there are a number of professional cutters who have set up in business for themselves, the Institutes might co-operate with one of these men and devise a real apprenticeship so that the work might live.

There are now numerous firms who make a speciality of supplying materials for this work. The Suffolk industry obtains skins from Somerset, the centre of the regular gloving industry. The Dunchurch makers buy from several different firms, since it has been found from experience that the best quality of each kind can be obtained from some particular firm. Suède, doeskin, and wash-leather are frequently used, and also ' cape ' and other coloured leathers. Some Institutes make rabbit fur gloves with knitted or leather palms.

Other leather work may conveniently be combined with glove-making, particularly if the organizer can devise ingenious methods of using up the small scraps which are unavoidably left when the gloves are cut out. Fancy girdles and other small articles can be made from these pieces and they can also be used for the trimmings of leather hats. A single worker in Lincolnshire has built up a successful spare-time industry, making gloves, bags, hats, and other small articles, chiefly of suède. Since these things, however, are more in the nature of luxuries than are the gloves, a wider market is needed for the disposal of them.

This leather-work is of a comparatively simple kind, the decoration of the articles being achieved mainly by the plaiting of narrow bands of leather, by cutting fringes, and by binding or sewing edges together with a strip of the leather as if it were a thread. Pieces of suède dyed in different colours are also combined effectively. Careful workmanship and ingenuity in designing new shapes and methods of decoration are the chief factors required for success. The craft is one which can easily be turned to account for the making of a great variety of gifts for friends, and thus it is one which is particularly suitable for Women's Institutes, provided that there is a sale for a certain amount of the work, for leather of all kinds is an expensive material, and no working woman could continue to buy supplies unless she were assured of a continual sale.

Another type of leather-work which is sometimes taken up by the Institutes is the decoration of bags, covers for books or blotters, and similar articles with stained and embossed patterns. Some beautiful work can be produced in this way and it has lately been very popular, and has been put on sale in some of the big London shops. But a talent for drawing and design is really a necessary asset to the successful worker in this craft. Special instruction is necessary and the material is particularly expensive, leather of a good grain and surface being required. The finished work is correspondingly dear, and is difficult to sell unless orders can be secured from a shop. It is also probable that any extensive demand for this type of work will prove to be but a passing fashion. There are numbers of individual workers, and those who have real talent find it a profitable occupation, but it does not lend itself to development as an industry.

In some Institutes various branches of fur-craft are practised, often in connexion with glove-making. The Herefordshire rabbitry supplies some very beautiful furs, particularly from rabbits of the Chinchilla and Beveren breeds, attractive in colouring and texture. The skins are made up into fur-lined suède slippers, collars, muffs, hats, and gloves, all being beautifully finished. The promoter of this industry gives lectures on curing and fur-craft in a number of Institutes in the neighbourhood. Skin-curing and fur-craft might perhaps be carried on successfully in many more Institutes and there should always be a good market for the work. In some counties, however, it is said to be difficult to find teachers and, where the workers have not the advantage, as in the above case, of a special local supply of skins, these are not easy to obtain in great quantities. Even when numbers of wild rabbits are killed locally, the skins are not available because the rabbits are all sent into the towns. If rabbits are to be specially bred a very great number would be required to supply a fur-craft industry of any size. The curing of the skins is rather a messy job, and many workers are perhaps more attracted by some craft for which the material may be bought ready for use without initial trouble. The curing of the skins of wild rabbits and making them up into gloves and slippers has been taught and is practised in a number of Institutes, but it is not carried on to any very great extent.

The Battlejack Cottage Industry has already been described as having grown out of the work of one old man who cured rabbit skins and made them into fur caps. It has now, however, developed into a factory industry and the skins are bought from the regular trade sources ready dressed.

Sheepskins, dressed with the wool on, are used for making mocassins. After the war a great quantity of these skins was available, having been prepared for making up into coats for the soldiers. There are one or two tanners who are specializing in the dressing of these skins for the use of handicraft workers, but many people complain that it is difficult to obtain them.

No instance has been found of the dressing and making up of moleskins as a home industry, although the wife of a mole-catcher who was learning fur-craft through Women's Institute classes was of the opinion that this might be

successfully developed. The skins are at their best throughout December and until the beginning of February. In
March the skins begin to be dark and blotchy on the inside,
which is a sign that the fur is poorer and will not wear so
well. When the weather is warm the moles have to be
skinned in the fields before being brought home, or the skins
may become entirely worthless. They are pinned on boards,
skin side uppermost, to dry, and stood in the open air if the
weather is fine. Under good conditions they will dry in
one night.

A mole-catcher in the Fen Country said that he sold the
best skins for 1s. 2d. in 1922 but that by March 1923 the price
had fallen to 8d. A Norfolk mole-catcher, however, at the
latter date stated that some of the skins still fetched as much
as 1s. 6d. They are graded into three classes and priced
accordingly. The mole-catchers sell them to furriers, who
dress them and make them up into coats, stoles, or other
articles. The skins vary greatly in colour and have to be
selected carefully, and the dressing and making up seems to
be an expensive process. In the case of any fur which
happens to be fashionable, as moleskin now is, the price
charged for the finished goods is an artificially inflated one.
But whilst the skins are so valuable it would probably be
difficult to obtain the supply necessary for the starting of
a village industry, particularly as a number might be damaged
by inexperienced workers in the early stages. The mole-
catcher depends for his living chiefly on the sale of the skins,
for the fee which is paid to him for the work of keeping the
land free from these alleged pests is a small one.

There is, however, a great extent of land on which no
fee is paid to a mole-catcher, and it is possible that a special
supply of skins could be obtained for an industry by employing a catcher. The mole-catcher's wife, who was particularly
interested in the development of fur-craft in the Women's
Institute, said that she often went out with her husband and
helped him in the work. But it is not a particularly pleasant
job and must be done at the most inclement seasons of the
year.

Rush-work. The first question to be considered in any
rush-working industry is whether locally grown raw material
can be utilized or whether the dried rushes are to be bought
from importers or dealers. Quantities of rushes and rush-
plait come from Holland and Belgium and these can be
sold so cheaply in England that most of the old native rush
industries here have either died out within recent years or

survive only in a small and precarious condition.[1] Nevertheless, some of the recently started village industries which
make use of rushes from a local source seem to find a good
sale for their work and to have fair prospects of further
development. Numbers of boys and girls were at one time
employed at rush-plaiting in many villages, and when this
type of labour was no longer available the higher wages which
must be paid to male workers were a factor in the decline
of the industry. The traditional making of horse collars
and mats is, where it is still carried on, done only by men,
and perhaps some of the heavier kinds of rush-work are not
suitable for women, but the plaiting of the narrower strips
and the braiding, weaving, or coiling of these to form small
bags or mats of various types, as well as the rush-seating of
chairs, is work which is easily done by women. The taste
and originality in design which some of the organizers of
these new industries have displayed must also have contributed to their success. In some cases dyed rushes have
been used, often to form a decorative border for mats, but
rush is a difficult material to dye successfully and considerable experience is needed. Since the natural brown, orange,
and green colourings of well harvested rushes are so attractive
this unnecessary elaboration of the craft seems rather
unfortunate, and it would be well to concentrate on the
drying of the rushes by the best methods, in order to preserve
their colour, and on selecting for each piece of work those
which harmonize.

The varieties of rushes and the ways in which they are
ordinarily used in the trade are described in another volume.[2]
Since the large rushes which are generally used grow in deep
running water the harvesting of them is not easy work, and
the handling of the bulky wet bunches when they are laid
out to dry is too heavy for women. One of the old rush-
cutters is therefore usually employed when the work is taken
up by a Women's Institute, but, since the qualifications for
the certificate of proficiency which is awarded by the Guild
of Learners includes a paper descriptive of the harvesting,
the members are encouraged to study the methods, with
a view to ensuring that the materials supplied to them are
properly dealt with. In North Hampshire a kind of river-
side sedge is used by Women's Institute workers in place of

[1] Compare vol. ii, *Osier Growing, Basketry Industries and Some Rural
Factories*, Part I; Chapter III, ' Rush, Sedge, and Reed Industries ', where
these industries are fully described.
[2] *ibid.*

rush. It is much finer than rush, is said to be more durable
when plaited in strands of a number of blades, and owing to
its light weight is suitable for hats. This material has one
great advantage over rush from the point of view of home
workers, in that it need not be used wet, for one of the drawbacks of rush-work is that the manipulation of long damp
rushes in the parlour does not add to the amenities of home
life in a small cottage. In Suffolk and Essex the Women's
Institute rush-workers use a three-cornered kind of sedge,
or ' segs ' as it is called locally, which grows in ditches where
it can easily be cut, and which has no pith and is therefore
quickly dried. Very little is known about the many kinds
of rush and sedge and the possible uses for them. Although
the old workers in the different districts where the rush
industry at one time flourished have considerable knowledge
about the local kinds which are useful, yet this traditional
lore is difficult to collate and apply, and the difficulty is
enhanced by the fact that the popular names, such as ' bul-
rush ', sedge, reed, &c., are applied to different plants in
different localities. There is clearly need for investigation
into this matter; on the lines of experiments with many kinds
of rushes, in the drying and weaving or braiding of them,
and of careful records of the work with botanical identifica-
tion of each variety. Some work of this kind is being done
by the Women's Institute workers in Suffolk and Essex, and
it is to be hoped that the results of their research will be
available to those who are dealing with rushes in other parts
of the country.

The Norfolk Institute workers braid the rushes into long
three-strand ropes, from which they make coiled mats,
large baskets for fire-wood, and waste-paper baskets with the
sides of a slender trellis-work of single rushes. In the Blandford industry the rushes are plaited and made into mats,
log-baskets, housemaids' kneelers, hassocks, which are also
stuffed with rush, and a variety of useful shopping baskets.
Similar work is done in Huntingdonshire, where, in addition,
oak stools and chairs, especially made for the Institute
workers, are seated with rushes. The hat-plaiting of the
North Hampshire Institutes is an experiment in a new direction, and for river or garden hats there seems to be considerable scope. There is some difficulty in getting good shapes,
but the plait can be sewn on to a buckram foundation which
is removed when the hat is finished. Decorative work can
be introduced, by plaiting, for example, a band or edge in
a different design, and it is important that this side of the

PLAITING RUSH BASKETS

SEDGE WORKERS AND THEIR PRODUCTS

Reproduced by kind permission of Miss W. G. Beddington

THE PRINCIPAL CRAFTS 97

work should be developed ; otherwise the hats may be bought and trimmed by others, who will receive all the credit and probably most of the cash, knowing the value of a foundation of hand-work better than the worker who has made it.

Straw-plaiting. Straw-plaiting is closely related to rush-work. As an industry it has been centred in the counties of Hertford, Bedford, and Essex since the seventeenth century, certain qualities in the wheat straw grown here rendering it particularly suitable for plaiting. The immense factory industry of hat-making, which has grown up in Luton and other towns in the straw-plaiting district, no longer obtains any considerable quantity of plait from local plaiters, most of the material used coming from abroad. It is not known whether, if the craft were to be revived for the purpose of making mats and light basketry, suitable straw could be obtained in other wheat-growing districts. At the present time straw-plaiting can hardly be spoken of as an industry apart from the small amount of out-work still done for the factories, which is described in another volume.[1] One woman in Essex, who was formerly an out-worker for a hat factory, has continued to practise the craft as an independent worker, selling through the Women's Institute the bags and baskets which she makes, but no other workers of this type have been met with. Nevertheless, there would appear to be possibilities for the further development of the craft if any organization were to take it up.

To obtain the straw it is necessary to make friends with a neighbouring farmer who can supply some of the proper colour and texture and who is willing to let the worker take it before threshing time, for straw which has been through the threshing machine is broken and useless for plaiting. The Essex woman buys ' a tidy lot ' for one shilling. Various processes must be carried out before the straw is ready for plaiting, such as the cutting of it into lengths free from knots, bleaching it, and, unless it is to be plaited whole, splitting and rolling it.[2] Tools are required for the last two processes, but they are small and of a simple kind, and numbers of them could probably be bought from the many women who have given up the work within the last twenty years. The straw can be dyed, but the pale golden outer side and the silvery inner side of the natural straw are very beautiful.

[1] Vol. ii, *Osier Growing, Basketry Industries and Some Rural Factories,* Part II, Chapter III, ' Outwork for Factories'.
[2] *Ibid.,* where these processes are described.

3203·2 H

If handicraft workers who are gifted with ingenuity in the application of simple material to novel decorative purposes would turn their attention to straw-plaiting and acquire from some of the old workers who still remain the necessary skill in plaiting the straws into many different patterns, a new and delightful home craft might be developed.

Another use for straw is found in the making of mats, which used to be part of the spare-time work of Suffolk farm labourers. Wheat straw is generally used, but rye straw or even hay will serve. The straw is taken in handfuls and plaited, three strands together, the plait being coiled as it is made to form a circular mat, and held together by threading one of the strands from time to time through the part already coiled. Another method was to braid the long plait first and then coil it, fastening it together with string, but this is less workmanlike. The mats were used on the floorboards of carts or in doorways, but unfortunately few men now make them. Wisps, or scrubbing brushes, are also made of straw.

Basketry. Basketry, with the use of either willow, cane, or raffia, is a favourite craft among Women's Institute workers and others. In certain counties the Institutes have taken up the making of willow baskets with considerable but misdirected zeal—misdirected because they are learning to make baskets of the type commonly produced by the ordinary village basket-maker, and, at a time when the latter is so hard put to it to earn a living, it is unfortunate than any organization which includes among its objects the promotion of rural industries should in this way contribute to the competition against which he is striving.

In one Institute, for example, about ten members were said to be working fairly steadily at basket-making. They had very little instruction. There was a demonstration, and then a few took a short course of instruction of a few weeks' duration and afterwards taught and helped the others. Shopping baskets, round, barrel-shaped, oval, and oblong, in white, buff, and brown, are the chief part of their output. The baskets seen were of indifferent workmanship, as might be expected under the circumstances. The weaving was generally too loose and open and the handles were not always secure. These ten workers probably made between them less than 100 baskets in a year, and perhaps this is well above the average output of an Institute which takes up the craft. The shopping basket is a variety which is sold chiefly in fancy shops, often being produced by a basket-maker who has several employees and who supplies the baskets at whole-sale prices to the shops. The work is of a kind which can be satisfactorily done by women and girls if they are properly trained, but in the trade no worker would be considered as really skilled, even in the making of a single type of basket, until she had worked for some months at least under the supervision of a man who had years of experience behind him. At the present time very few English makers can produce this type of basket at a cost low enough to compete success-fully with the foreign baskets which are now more commonly seen in the shops.

A Lincolnshire Institute, when visited in 1922, was taking up the making of potato picking baskets, a very unsuitable type of work for women, for strong, coarse rods are used which are rough and hard to manipulate. A certain amount of willow basketry is done by Institute workers in nearly every county, although in many cases very little work is made for sale.

The question of competition with the regular trade hardly arises in the case of *cane* basket-making by women home workers. There are in Warwickshire two women who, having taken up the making of cane baskets in the first instance through the Women's Institute and as a hobby, are now carrying it on as at least a partial livelihood. The work they do is original and unlike the usual types of English basketry. All kinds of baskets for domestic use, such as for firewood, cut flowers, waste paper, or for shopping, as well as chairs, cradles, &c., are made of cane dyed by the workers in bright colours. Cane is easier to manipulate than willow rods, being softer and more pliant, and therefore the work is more suitable for women. The fact that considerable strength of hand is needed in making willow baskets, to put the rods into place and keep the weaving close in texture, probably accounts for the inferiority of the women's work in this material. The quality of willow depends very much upon the methods of cultivation employed, so that the success of a willow basket-making industry is involved with willow growing, in which long experience and great technical knowledge are required. But all cane is imported and there are many dealers who have specialized in the selection of the kinds most suitable for handicraft workers, so that the latter may obtain this material on terms as good as those on which any small basket-maker buys it, and are not, as compared with him, at the disadvantage from which they suffer when buying willows, of the cultivation of which they

H 2

know nothing. There is also great scope for original decorative work in cane basketry, and women, with their deftness of fingers, easily excel men at this craft. Nevertheless, it does not seem to have been taken up very extensively by Women's Institutes or other individual workers, although, in addition to the two already mentioned, there are several others who make various types of small fancy baskets and weave cane edgings on wooden trays. Probably the greater cost of the material, as compared with willow, has been a difficulty, but if this could be met, there should be an opening for the further development of the industry.

Raffia work is of a different type from cane and willow basketry, although it is sometimes done on a foundation of cane, which gives the stiffness lacking in raffia. A great variety of articles can be made and there is infinite scope for the ingenuity of clever workers. Raffia, being very soft and pliable, is easily worked, although experience is needed to know the exact state of dampness in which it should be used. Although it is very popular as a craft practised chiefly to provide things for the worker's own use and for presents to her friends, yet the amount of work which goes to the making of many articles, especially of the closely woven type, makes it somewhat difficult to sell the things at a price which repays the maker adequately.

Mats and Rugs. There are many types of mats and rugs which are made by handicraft workers, including the members of Women's Institutes. The woven strips of rush matting, the thick mats of coiled rush-plait, and the straw mats have already been mentioned. A mat which can be made as a bye-product by any one who has a hand-loom of moderate size is that in which narrow strips of coloured rag (any scraps of cotton material) are knotted together into a long string and woven through a string warp. This forms a cheap but durable mat, easily cleaned or even washed, and of pleasant appearance if the materials are sorted out with discrimination.

Another kind of mat made of scraps of material cut into long strips is very popular among country women in the north of England. The groundwork is of canvas and the narrow pieces of material, cut as long as possible, are threaded with a needle in and out of the canvas, leaving upstanding loops on the right side of the mat. Any kind of material can be used, even old stockings, cut up spirally into long strips, being very useful, and if suitable stuff is used the mat can easily be washed. It is said to be far more sanitary than the old-fashioned ' progged ' mat which is still universally popular, but which is really a horrible dust-trap. This kind of mat is made of three-cornered pieces of material, generally cloth, which are threaded into the canvas, with the loose ends forming the pile ; they are therefore rougher and shaggier than the others, which have no loose ends, but only the small loops of tightly folded stuff.

Yet another variety of mat which is made by many country women in the north utilizes the short pieces of ' michael string ', the binder twine which is cut from each sheaf of corn at the threshing. It is threaded into canvas in the same way as the long folded strips of stuff, and makes a mat which, in colour and appearance, resembles those of coco-nut fibre. Long strips of this matting may often be seen in a country kitchen, laid down to save the floor from the marks of muddy boots.

The wool rug is one of the things most commonly made by Women's Institute workers. Short lengths of coarse wool are knotted on to canvas, and patterns can be worked out in wools of different colours.

Three types of mats seem to be characteristic of Suffolk. One is the straw mat already described, another is a mat made by fishermen and lighthouse keepers, of manilla twine fastened in spirals upon a groundwork of sail-cloth, while the third is made of strips of cotton material, old summer dresses or worn sheets, cut up and dyed, the strips plaited tightly and then coiled and sewn together, as in making mats of rush-plait.

All these mats are chiefly made by cottage women for use in their own homes, but some are occasionally made for sale, particularly the wool rugs, which are often sold at Women's Institute exhibitions. The initial outlay on material and the time needed to produce the finished article being so much greater than in the case of gloves, fewer members do the wool rug work, but some excellent rugs are made. A woman who can only give one or two hours a day to the work will take many weeks to make a rug, but the mats made of folded strips of material threaded through canvas can be finished in a week. These also are sometimes sold, and it might be better to teach the making of these simpler kinds in Institutes, in districts where they are not already known, than of the wool rugs, for which few women can afford the necessary outlay on material (£2–£3) or are ready to work for so long before they can see the complete result of their labour.

Needlework, Embroidery, and Kindred Crafts. All branches

of needlework are encouraged by the Women's Institutes, and in some cases some particular work, such as the making of children's clothing, has been developed. Wherever there is an Institute handicraft shop the village women who can do fine work may find a sale for it.

Needlework industries are carried on in several places with success, particularly when the work has some distinctive character. The Bloxworth sunbonnet industry is an example, frocks, overalls, and jumpers as well being made there. The Lytchett Minster button industry, which at one time employed six workers, had dwindled, in 1921, to a single one. Probably this particular craft would be more likely to flourish in connexion with an industry for making frocks or jumpers on which the buttons could be used. They were worked in silk on small rings.

Of embroidery industries the one founded at Fisherton-de-la-Mere for crippled workers, male and female, is among the most notable. The work is modelled on old embroideries and is done on hand-made linen, unbleached or sun-bleached, in unbleached or white linen thread. The designs are beautiful in themselves and suitable to the material used, and the care exercised in teaching and the high standard insisted on produce excellent results. The industry, which has flourished for some thirty years, proves that, with proper training, skill in the finest work can be attained by the most unpromising people, men and women alike.

The prospects are uncertain for the filet-lace-making industry at Rushmore, although the work is beautiful. The advantages of this work for a home industry are the fact that very little outlay is needed and the making of the nets, which are the foundation of the work, is easily learnt. As the workers become more skilled they learn the embroidery of patterns on the net, which is interesting although simple work, with scope for originality of design.

At certain Women's Institute exhibitions there has been an excellent sale for knitted gloves at good prices, and it has been suggested that some of the old knitters whose employment as outworkers for the Ringwood glove industry [1] has ceased might, as members of Women's Institutes, obtain help in buying materials and find a means of selling their work. This is a useful occupation for elderly women whose sight is failing, but is probably not capable of development into an industry for large numbers of workers.

[1] Described in vol. ii, *Osier Growing, Basketry Industries and Some Rural Factories*, Part II, Chapter III, ' Outwork for Factories '.

An interesting branch of the needlework industries is the *quilting* which is a traditional craft in Northumberland and other counties in the north of England. The quilts are very large and heavy, with a wadding of cotton wool, the decoration consisting of stitching in the same colour as the material, worked in wavy lines or conventional angular shapes. Some of the designs are said to date from the time of Queen Elizabeth, and their names—' feathers ', ' beehive ', ' bellows '— show from what simple objects the units of the patterns are derived. In many of the designs these simple elements are combined to produce an elaborate effect. The making of one quilt is a long and laborious task, one worker stating that if two women were to sit at it for eight hours a day it would take them a fortnight or three weeks to complete. The quilts are chiefly made for use at home, but are also sold occasionally. They are said to be particularly popular in coal-mining districts, but are often to be seen in the farmhouses of Northumberland.

Toy-making. Soft toys have been made by a great many Women's Institute members, but although during the war there was often a good sale for the toys at Christmas time, it is now generally found to be very difficult to sell them at a price which repays the workers. Thus the work, taken up with enthusiasm in some counties, has now languished, although a few toys may still be made for the worker's own children and for friends. Two Yorkshire villages were still finding a good sale for their toys in 1922, and in 1923 there were some excellent specimens shown in the sale-room of the Home Arts and Industries Association, which would probably find a ready sale because of the originality of their design and the care with which the shapes had been worked out. One village industry produced a very popular duck, made of towelling and yellow material and stuffed with cork so that it would float in the bath. In the stereotyped patterns handicraft workers cannot compete with factory-made toys, but if good new designs are made and carefully executed there seems to be some chance of disposing of the toys at Christmas time. Too often the work is clumsy, careless, and distorted, as a result of which lop-sided creatures are produced which one would be reluctant to give to any child.

The making of wooden toys has not yet been taken up by the Institutes to any great extent, but there are a number of other groups of workers producing them. Small carved and painted models in delightful designs have been seen, but they are generally the work of one or two artists working together, who have hardly developed anything which could be called a village industry. A Sussex ' wood tug ', or tree-hauling tackle, was one of the most effective products of one worker in that county. A hunt, complete with hounds, huntsman, whips, and field, is an attractive set made by another group of workers.

Fretwork figures, cut out of flat pieces of wood and painted, are more easily made by workers with little artistic talent, as the design can be marked out on the wood and no carving is needed. A more skilled worker can paint the figures. If the designs are good and new ones are constantly thought of, these figures are readily sold in handicraft shops and wholesale orders can be obtained. Many disabled ex-service men have taken up the work. One of these said that he had received, during the few weeks before Christmas, far more orders than he and his family could carry out.

Shoe- and Slipper-making. In addition to leather moccasin work, there are several kinds of shoe- and slipper-making which can conveniently be taken up as home industries. The ' Longleat shoes ' are made of canvas, with crotcheted string soles, interlined with linoleum. Patterns cut out in wood with a fret-saw were obtained from a good boot-maker in London. The cutting of the linoleum is done by one worker, and others make up the shoes. Materials have proved expensive and difficult to obtain. The twine comes from Ireland and the canvas from a shoe manufacturer at Leicester. Variations in materials and method are intro-duced. Some slippers are made of felt, others are lined with warm material. Raffia is used for bedroom slippers. The sewing is done by hand (although some might be done on a machine), and decorative stitchery could be employed. A simpler way of making the soles is to use thicker twine and sew it straight on to the sole, round and round in one piece, so that the strands lie close together as in the Spanish canvas shoes.

Slipper-making, being easy and comparatively cheap to carry out, is an excellent home craft for countrywomen, enabling them, as it does, to supply their children with slippers. During the war it was extremely popular, and although it is found that there is less sale for the slippers now, yet it is a craft which the workers would do well to keep up if only to supply their own families. In some villages a piece of good community work has been done in the making of a supply of slippers for the school children, to enable them to take off their wet boots. It would be a good plan for the Women's Institutes to try to make their crafts definitely supplementary to the local trade crafts, rather than competitive. Thus, the cobbling which is sometimes taught in the Institute classes is very helpful in small villages where there is no shoemaker, and to women who cannot afford to supply their children with a second pair of boots, so that the one pair must be mended on Saturday or at night when the children are not at school. Yet the village cobbler and bootmaker should be encouraged (and particularly so since a great many ex-service men have been trained in this trade), for he can obtain properly tanned leather and make strong durable boots and shoes, far more suited to country wear than the factory products of poor materials which are sold in the cheaper shops. Therefore any movement to take work out of the hands of the village cobbler would be a misdirected one. The making of light house slippers should benefit his trade, by helping the wearers to save their boots and to buy better ones which would be more worth repairing.

Amongst other crafts which may be mentioned here, *Papier mâché* is popular among the Women's Institutes in some counties. The cost of material is small, but this is rather messy work, and a special work-room is really needed to undertake it satisfactorily. Some attractive bowls have been seen, decorated by the skilful use of coloured paper. Thus a bowl made of grocers' blue paper bags had stripes of orange paper. The bowls can be rendered watertight if they are well made and enamelled or varnished.

Metal-work. The iron scroll-work done in Salisbury, including the making of gates, fire-irons, and candlesticks, involves the use of a forge and is really a branch of smithing, requiring more technical training than most of the work described in this chapter and being more suited to a regular than to a part-time or home industry. The hammered, or 'raised', and the repoussé work are, however, of a simpler kind and easily learnt. They are carried on by many evening classes for boys and men, and are used for caskets, trays, bowls, candlesticks, and other articles.

Brass or bronze, copper and silver are all used for this work. The repoussé work is the easier and requires less plant. In a typical village metal industry there are two work-rooms, in one of which there is accommodation at tables for about twelve men doing repoussé work. The patterns are traced on the metal by means of carbon paper and then pressed out with the tools. There is a good deal of noise here when a number of men are at work, but it is nothing to the resounding din which fills the other workshop devoted to hammered or raised work, where there are a furnace, anvils, and a hand-drill. Flat sheets of metal are hammered on a stake or anvil, the concavity being gradually beaten out when bowls, the holders of candlesticks, and other curved pieces are made. At Chipping Campden, stakes curved to the required shape and made in the neighbouring forge (where ornamental iron-work is also produced) are used to work on, being held firmly in a vice. Considerable skill is required to keep hammered work level and even, and more time is needed than for the repoussé work, so that it is correspondingly expensive, but there is generally a better sale for it. The hammer, with its highly polished surface, gives a certain amount of polish to the metal, which has to be put into the fire to be annealed many times during the beating out of each bowl or holder. A skilled worker can evolve the design of whatever he is working on as he gradually hammers it out and the slight indentations made by the hammer all over the surface form the only decoration.

iii. *The Workers.*

Since a great deal of the work described here under the heading of ' home crafts and industries ' is done less as a livelihood than as a spare-time occupation or a supple-mentary employment, it follows that a great number of the workers are women, who often carry on a home craft in the time they can spare from household duties. In reviewing the different types of work and the people who do them, it is clearly seen that many of the distinctions often made between men's and women's work are quite artificial. Of course, the particular crafts here considered, being of the kind suitable for home industries, are comparatively light and simple and do not involve the manipulation of heavy tools or elaborate machinery. Many of them are equally suitable for children or for young girls and lads. The Fisherton-de-la-Mere embroidery industry for cripples illustrates again the fact, often demonstrated during the war and since, when occupation must be found for disabled soldiers, that men can achieve and can take pleasure in the most delicate needlework, and it may be recalled that some of the old lace-makers were men. On the other hand, although all the work in the metal industries investigated is done by men—with the exception of that of the silversmith near Honiton who is helped by his wife—yet it is likely that there is an opening for the development of this kind of work among women. The proprietors of the copper-beating shop at Hayle stated that there would be room for a number of girls here if capital were available for the extension of the business. At Heversham, in the Lake District, the teacher of the metal-working classes is a woman, and there are certainly a number of individual craftswomen in different parts of the country who do repoussé metal-work, pewter work being one of the activities of Women's Institutes in at least one county. It is found that the fingers of boys under eleven are not strong enough for metal-work, and when the classes are carried on under the auspices of the Home Arts and Industries Association the boys must leave at the age of sixteen to learn a regular trade, although a cripple unfit for other work may be kept on, and the others may return later to do part-time work.

Rush-plaiting is an example of a craft which, although in the regular trade it is now done only by men, has been very successfully taken up by women as a handicraft, and has in at least one case been carried on by a woman for a livelihood. Boys and girls used to be employed in great numbers in the regular trade, and one old marshman, an experienced rush-worker, who had taught the craft to women, expressed the opinion that they were better at it than men, having smaller and quicker fingers. In fact the prospects for rush-plaiting as a home craft are brighter than those for the regular industry.

Two objections are often raised to the usefulness of the craft-teaching work of such organizations as the Women's Institutes. One is that the average village woman has little inclination to learn craft-work, or, even if she is keen to learn, has little ability in any such work; another, that in any case it is never satisfactory to learn a craft late in life, and such people as the old lace-makers, who have been brought up in the stern tradition that a girl must be trained to work at the pillow at the tender age of five or six, will uphold this theory and sometimes speak scornfully of the present-day classes for older girls and women. Examples of failure in attempts to interest village people in handicraft work can be quoted to bear out these contentions, but an even greater number of outstanding successes can also be found, and there are bound to be many mistakes made in a new movement such as this. The flourishing Women's Institute industry at Dunchurch in Warwickshire, which produces excellent work in several different crafts and finds a ready sale for it, proves that village women are capable of becoming skilled craftswomen in a year or so, even when they have done none of this kind of work in their childhood, for it is the ordinary cottage members who are the mainstay of this industry. The idea is widely accepted that craft-skill is inherited, and as a proof of this theory it is pointed out that, for example, a child descended from generations of pillow-lace makers will learn lace-making more easily and will have a better ' touch ' than another child. It is difficult to say, however, whether there is really any inherited manual dexterity and delicacy of touch, or whether the child, even though she was not taught to make lace by her mother, has not acquired almost unconsciously a familiarity with the technique of the craft through watching her mother at work. The arts and crafts movement does not seem to have produced any evidence up to the present to confirm the theory of inherited craft-skill. It so happens that there has been no outstanding attempt to start a new handicraft industry in the pillow-lace district. If the country people of the Lake District really showed more aptitude for weaving and spinning, when these were revived amongst them by Ruskin's followers, it may have been due to the fact that these crafts were at that time hardly extinct as home industries and many of the workers had already learnt them or watched their parents practise them. As a matter of fact the revived industry does not seem to have taken any firm root amongst the working-class people of the district, and although it is still carried on there, few of the agricultural population are employed in it. Many of the newer handicraft industries have been started successfully in districts where there is no tradition or survival of ancient craft-work, as, for instance, in Warwickshire. It is possible that the descendants of the pillow-lace makers would learn a new craft more quickly than the Warwickshire women and attain to greater skill, and any enterprise which would put this to the test would be interesting.

The experience of individual craft-workers who have tried to train village boys and girls as employees is interesting. A maker of cane baskets, who had had three girls from the village working with her for some time, found them useful on the unskilled or semi-skilled work, such as dyeing and preparing the cane and doing some work on the bottoms of the baskets (the least skilled process in the actual weaving), but said that they needed constant supervision. She had not, however, really been able to afford to give the time required to train a girl thoroughly. A glove-maker in Lincolnshire declared that she could not persuade any other woman in the village to take up the work seriously, although she herself often had more orders than she could cope with and would have been glad of a helper. In this county it was said that the only women who had had much success in the making of gloves for sale were former tailoresses or dressmakers, and that generally the village women did not attain to any great skill. Toy-makers in a Sussex village told the same tale, that their attempt to train boys and girls to carve wooden toys had not been successful, as the pupils were so slow and wasted so much material. This particular work, however, requires more skill than many of the crafts chosen for village industries. The designer of the toys is an artist, and some innate artistic ability would be necessary in any one who was to become a successful carver. In the various metal-working industries there seems to be no difficulty in inducing a number of village men and boys to spend several evenings a week regularly at the work, but of course it is to them more in the nature of a pastime than an employment, and the amount earned is small. In Women's Institutes, also, handicraft work is, in the first instance, taken up as a recreation, although an industry with part-time workers may be developed. Probably the success of an industry which grows up in this way depends partly upon the fact that the workers take up the craft to begin with simply because it interests them, and not because they are looking for ' a job '.

In many cases such simple work as plain sewing or knitting and the sewing of gloves is given out by a handicraft shop, a glove industry, or a group of craft-workers, to village women and girls, and as a rule there seems to be no difficulty in finding workers. Perhaps the Lincolnshire glove-maker's trouble was due to the fact that she sought not only a woman who would sew for her but someone with sufficient enterprise to become a co-operator in the industry.

It is likely that workers who would be interested in a craft and would soon achieve skill in it could be found in any village, provided that the enterprise was started on the right lines as regards the two important points of teaching and organization.[1] Good methods of both are to be found in the Women's Institute movement.

[1] It is possible, however, that in districts where the women do a great deal of work on the land, craft-work as a part-time occupation would never be very popular ; there is less need for the additional income.

The organizers have aimed at providing good teachers who can not only do good work themselves but understand how to impart their knowledge to others. They also try to keep the attention of each Institute centred on one craft, since it is thus easier to provide teachers, and the members, as well, help each other considerably by comparison of their achievements and ideas. Weekly working parties are held by some Institutes in addition to the ordinary monthly meeting, and the importance of a good work-room for the craftswomen is realized. When the workers have been sufficiently discouraged from their tendency to draw their only ideas of design from the commonplace transfers sold in fancy shops, and when they have learned to accept criticism in the right spirit and gained the courage to undo a piece of bad work and start it over again, they begin to do really good original work. This stage is only reached after a slow uphill struggle, but undoubtedly some of the workers have attained to it.

The Women's Institute organization provides special facilities for this method of gradually arousing interest in craft-work. It is probable that many attempts at organizing handicraft industries in country districts fail through the impatience of the promoters, who do not realize that it is not only necessary to teach the bare technique of the craft, but, more important still, to arouse in these country people who have had little or no artistic training at school a real understanding of the principles of craftsmanship and that ' infinite capacity for taking pains ' which, whether or no it is the characteristic of a genius, is certainly that of the craftsman. It is curious that in a village where men have for generations been carrying out with care and exactness the dozen or more skilled processes which go to the making of a rake, or the deft and rhythmical movements which shape a flower-pot, the products of a factory should be regarded as the finest achievement of civilization, while hand-work is considered hardly worth troubling about. Yet there still remain in our English villages men and women in whom such skill as that of the potter or rake-maker may be developed, together with, in rarer cases, the freedom of design based, not on any stereotyped pattern, but on the nature of the material worked in and the use to which it is to be put. These qualities have produced the beautiful and admirably suitable things which many village craftsmen are still making, the various types of farm wagon, the quaint local baskets, such as Sussex trugs, Cumberland swills, Southport ' boats ', the earthenware pitchers and bowls made in old-fashioned potteries, and innumerable other things. The same qualities should produce new things of as beautiful design in the future. The workers in home crafts and industries who have already been written of in this section are, for the most part, drawn from the rural population. The Chipping Campden craftsmen, however, are an exception in that many of them were originally drawn from the regular town trades and, whilst the guild was situated in London, these skilled silver-smiths, wood-carvers, and other craftsmen found it easy to return to the commercial firms at times when the guild was in low water, although they were glad to come back to the guild when that was possible, on account of the greater freedom of design allowed to them in their work there. This policy of taking craftsmen already trained in ordinary trade methods does not seem to have been continued, and in late years a number of lads, some from Campden itself, have been trained in the guild workshops, about sixteen of them being employed there when the place was visited in March 1922.

Special industries for the disabled, and the special problems connected with them, have already been mentioned. In addition to the disabled ex-service men there are at all times a proportion of crippled, blind, and slightly mentally deficient people who can, if they are taught crafts, contribute to their own support and whose unfortunate lot can be considerably mitigated when some interest, such as is supplied by a craft, is introduced into their lives. Industries for the disabled cannot, as a rule, be entirely self-supporting, even when a great deal of teaching and organization is done by voluntary workers. Being infirm and, therefore, usually incapable of a regular and reliable output, many of the workers, even if they lived in a place well situated for getting work, would be practically ineligible for employment in a commercial firm. The regulation of wages and hours makes it more difficult for firms to employ workers from whom they cannot be sure of a certain output punctually delivered. Those who teach sub-normal workers need also special skill and patience, and, indeed, the success of any industry for such workers depends largely upon the personal qualities of the teachers and organizers. It is therefore probable that home industries on a small scale will always play an important part in the provision of employment for the disabled, many of whom are capable of excellent crafts-manship under careful supervision, although their rate of work is always slower than that of ordinary workers.

The earnings of handicraft workers in their own homes or in small workshops vary a great deal according to the methods of organizing the work, the aims of the promoters, the facilities for the sale of the work, and other factors. Very low rates of payment are, unfortunately, sometimes a characteristic of small village industries run from so-called ' philanthropic ' motives, and the promoter of such an industry is sometimes able to impress the workers so forcibly with the idea of her philanthropy that they will toil uncomplainingly for a wage which would rouse the most passive of employees in a commercial industry to strong protest. In such cases the promoter does not usually reap any profits from the enterprise, as, either the goods are sold at too low a price, or, more often, the industry, owing to bad organization, will not yield higher wages to the workers.

Home industries can be compared, in the matter of wages, with out-work for factories and with the lace industry, all possessing the common characteristic that the work is done at home in the workers' spare time and must therefore be paid for by piece rates. Whilst the industry does not have to bear the expense of renting premises and lighting and heating them, on the other hand, production is irregular and there are additional expenses in distributing and collecting the work. The payment for the various forms of out-work before the war ranged usually from 1d. to 2d. an hour, but of course these rates have risen considerably since that time. During 1921 and 1922, when most of these investigations were made, £1 per week was the amount earned by many out-workers who spent the greater part of their time on the work, although many earned less. Lace-making is, of course, notoriously poorly paid, and in 1922 the average earnings of fourteen typical cases were just over 1¾d. an hour. The earnings in the better organized home industries, so far as they can be estimated, generally compare favourably with such examples as these. One woman who made raffia baskets for sale, and who was also a lace-maker, declared that on the closely woven work in raffia she could not earn more than 2d. an hour, about the same amount as she could earn by lace-making, although raffia baskets in the more open and quickly woven pattern could be sold at relatively higher prices. Raffia work of this kind is, however, not likely to become very profitable, unless, perhaps, in cases where the worker finds a very good market and makes articles of a striking originality in design. Obviously the making of a very closely woven raffia basket occupies a great deal of time in relation to the result achieved, and few people are willing to pay a high price for such a basket when one of cane, more quickly made because of a coarser material, would serve their purpose. In some cases the low rate of payment to the workers is due simply to the inefficient organization of the industry. In a certain small glove industry, carried on in connexion with a Women's Institute, the workers were paid 2s. 6d. for making a pair of suède or wash-leather gloves—a wage of about 2d. an hour. No regular market for the gloves had been found, there seemed to be no system for fixing the selling prices, and the workers were discontented. In other Women's Institutes glove industries, better organized, the workers' earnings are more satisfactory. In one case where a regular industry is carried on, the excellent plan is followed of having two or three grades of payment fixed for every piece of work, according to the quality of the workmanship. Thus the highest rate paid for sewing a pair of plain suède gauntlet gloves was 3s. 6d., whilst the worker received 6d. or 1s. less if the work was inferior. In another county the Institute glove-makers were selling their output in 1922 at from 4s. to 5s. per pair above the cost of material, which they considered to be equivalent to a rate of about 4d. an hour for cutting out and sewing the gloves. In the former case, where 3s. 6d. per pair was paid to the workers, the selling price was fixed by the addition of a percentage to cover the running expenses of the industry. A small profit had been made and paid into the Institute funds.

In one County Federation of Women's Institutes the plan was adopted of pricing all handicraft work which was sold on the basis of a rate of 6d. an hour for the work, the worker being instructed to time herself. This sort of standard is very difficult of application, since the skill of the workers varies considerably, many of them being very inexperienced, and also because a great deal of the work is done in spare time during a number of separate short periods. Thus, owing to the worker's inability to concentrate on the work for long at a time, it would be done at a slow pace and she could not expect to earn such high rates as a regular worker. The rate of 6d. an hour seems in this case to have fixed the selling price too high for the market, for although a certain amount of work could be sold at local shows, some specimens of rush-work which were sent to the Country Industries Trading Society were stated by that organization to be priced 33⅓ per cent. too highly.

The earnings of workers in the Bloxworth sunbonnet industry were estimated in 1921 at about 4*d*. an hour, the three regular workers having earned during the year ending June 1920 the total sums of £20 10*s*. 8*d*., £33 18*s*. 4*d*., and £18 15*s*. 3*d*. respectively. The women making the nets for filet-lace at Rushmore were, at the same period, earning 6*d*. an hour, whilst those who did the embroidery could earn rather more. The button industry at Lytchett Minster used to bring in an average of £10 a year to half a dozen workers, but had dwindled considerably when visited in 1921. The workers in another of the numerous small village industries in the south-west of England, the Longleat shoemaking, have earned sums ranging from 7*s*. 6*d*. to 30*s*. a week.

Two metal-working enterprises which are run more on the lines of trade workshops than of home industries pay their regular workers at ordinary trade rates. At Newlyn it was stated that the rates are based on the usual earnings in similar trades, but the workers also receive a proportion of the profits. In the Sarum iron works the men are paid by time rates, the employer considering that artistic work is not suitable for piece rates, and the wages are rather above the general average of wages in the town. In the Newton metal industry the workers, farm labourers who spend two or three evenings a week in the workshop during the winter months, earn about 4*d*. an hour on all their work that is sold. The metal industries in the Lake District, which are run on similar lines, bring in about £10 or £11 a year to the workers for two or three evenings a week, a rate of perhaps about 3*d*. or 4*d*. an hour.

From these examples it can be seen that the earnings vary rather according to the organization of the industry than according to the skill required in the work. It must be borne in mind that men or women who can only spare short periods of time for craft-work in the intervals of other occupations cannot expect to earn wages which will represent a high rate per hour. Even an expert worker can achieve much less in six separate half-hour periods than in three hours of uninterrupted work, and the more irregular the work the lower the earnings are likely to be. Many of these village industries have as yet hardly grown beyond the experimental stage. They are still feeling for markets, their output is still irregular, which adds to the difficulty of sale, their workers are inexperienced and they steer a perilous course between the Scylla of too high a payment to the workers, which will raise the selling price beyond commercial limits, and the Charybdis of paying them so poorly that no one will wish to do the work. As industries are developed, the workers will realize the value of organization, not only of the whole business, but of each individual worker's methods, and of setting aside certain times for the craft-work in stretches of two or three hours whenever possible. The lace-makers have long ago been driven by hard necessity to realize the value of this, and although few of them can reckon up how many hours a day they give to the work, nevertheless it is clear from a number of visits paid at random to many old lace-makers who rely on their earnings for part of their livelihood, that it is their custom to arrange their house-work so that they may have two or three hours of steady work at the pillow before their midday meal, and again another hour or so—after the rest necessary when very fine work is being done—whilst the precious daylight lasts. Some of the promoters of home industries fail to encourage regular work because they think it is so much more pleasant for the workers to be able to ' pick up the work at odd moments ', but this system, or rather lack of system, does not make for good workmanship, and, whilst it keeps down the rate of earnings, it lessens the chances that the worker will attain to any skill in original design, for which concentration is essential. The steady attention which the lace-makers have been forced to give to their work has produced true craftswomen, who delight in the work for its own sake and in spite of the wretched payment which they receive for it.

iv. *Markets.*

It has already been pointed out that the majority of home handicraft workers need to find some special channel through which to put their goods on the market, since ordinary trade methods are usually unsuitable for them. One reason for this is that the value of handicraft work lies to a great extent in its individuality and any attempt at mass production such as would be required if the trade were to be supplied would detract from this value. A few big London shops and one or two in the provinces buy some of the output of individual handicraft workers, but it is often found in these cases that the very large percentage which these retailers must add to the maker's price to cover their expenses and profit, keeps the producer's price very low, and the things can be more advantageously sold to some small local handi-craft shop whose overhead expenses are smaller. Artist-

I 2

craftsmen declare that the tendency on the part of 'the trade' to beat down the price to the lowest possible limit militates against the maker's aim of doing the very best work. The Chipping Campden Guild at one time had its own shop in Bond Street, but although the sales were good the great expense of running the shop caused the enterprise to be abandoned.

As a general rule the best market for handicraft work is to be found in the small shops specializing in goods of this kind, which are becoming increasingly numerous in country towns and in the suburbs of London, and in the annual handicraft exhibitions organized in London and large towns by the craft-workers' societies, particularly the Home Arts and Industries Association. The Women's Institutes hold their own exhibitions and have stalls at local shows, and handicraft workers sometimes join an Institute mainly for the sake of the opportunity thus afforded for the sale of their work. Private orders received through friends and then through a gradually widening circle of acquaintances, provide a market for many individual workers whose output is not large.

These exhibitions are, however, often organized only with the help of voluntary work or of contributions of money, and the industries which rely on this method of sale cannot be considered as entirely self-supporting. The exhibitions are of value also for the opportunity they afford for comparison of work and exchange of ideas, but this educational value, as well as the interest of the exhibition, would be greatly increased if the ordinary village 'trades', such as those of the brush-, basket-, and rope-makers, the potters and turners, could also be represented as well as the newer enterprises the work of which is, rather artificially, generally distinguished as 'craft-work'. A stall at a handicraft exhibition might prove a valuable form of advertisement for the small village 'tradesman', who can only continue to exist by producing something distinctly better than the output of the competing factories. Moreover, the gulf which unfortunately exists between the new 'Arts and Crafts' movement and the older industries might in this way be bridged and both parties would be benefited, educationally for certain, and probably financially.

Another criticism which may be made of the Arts and Crafts exhibitions is that, whilst they lay stress on hand-work as such, they do not always make it a rule that the actual makers, throughout all the processes of the work shown, should be made known. Thus, one weaver may show material for which she has dyed and spun the yarn as well as having woven it on a hand-loom, while another may show material hand-woven from machine-spun and factory dyed yarns. Exhibitors show as their own work papier mâché or wooden bowls which they have only decorated by painting or staining, or pottery which they obtain as biscuit ware from a local commercial pottery works, paint, and then return to the works for baking. Rush hats, woven by home workers, may be trimmed and exhibited by a second worker. The handicraft workers are apt to criticize ordinary trade on the grounds that the actual worker does not become known to the buyer, but in these cases the same conditions are found in the arts and crafts movement.

Some of the societies which arrange these exhibitions have already been mentioned. In addition to these the Red Rose Guild of Art-workers, with head-quarters in Manchester, holds exhibitions, chiefly for workers in the north of England. The annual ' Englishwoman Exhibition ' in London always shows a great variety of craft-work. Many counties, particularly in the south-west of England, have their Arts and Crafts societies, such as those of Wiltshire, Dorset, Hampshire, and Devon, and these may, by affiliation to the Home Arts and Industries Association, make the work of their exhibitors known further afield.

The method of sale by private orders through the post is, of course, not suitable for all kinds of craft-work, but is found to be practicable in the case of such things as gloves and embroidery, which can easily be sent through the post. A glove-maker living in a remote corner of Lincolnshire showed her work at a Glasgow exhibition organized by the London Craft-workers' Group, and in this way obtained many orders, some of them from shops. This encouraged her to ask for orders from shops in other towns, and she sold some work in this way in Hull and Scunthorpe. By these orders and through her friends she sold over £80 worth of goods during 1922, including 80 leather bags, 60 pairs of gloves, and a number of leather hats and small articles. Another glove-maker in the same county, but working quite separately, sold nearly 200 pairs of gloves in a year. Her husband was a mechanic in a factory in Lincoln and she obtained orders through her friends, her husband's workmates and people introduced by them, so that her earnings by glove-making were a valuable addition to her income whilst he was out of work for some months. Sometimes she had more orders than she could cope with. One special order, received from an institution, was for gloves of peculiar shapes to fit crippled people. Again, from Women's Institute glove-makers in the south-western counties the report comes that in 1921 there was a good sale of the work through personal acquaintances and private orders. A few local shops were also supplied, but there was little attempt to sell wholesale, for while the standard varies so much from worker to worker a wholesale trade in articles which depend so much on exactitude in cut and size would be impracticable even if it were desired. In some cases makers in remote villages have experienced difficulty in establishing a connexion with customers, especially in a district where there are few people of the richer classes, but it seems that, once the makers achieve a high standard of work, they can risk the necessary outlay on a stall at an exhibition with a reasonable certainty of a good number of orders as a result.

Different types of work have their own particular advantages or difficulties in relation to the market. Toys, for instance, unlike many of the handicraft products, seem to be readily saleable through the ordinary trade channels ; the reason probably being that, since the chief demand for them is a seasonal one, the maker does not need to produce large quantities at short notice, but can make on stock throughout the year and sell the whole output before Christmas. So long as the maker is not under the financial necessity of securing steady returns throughout the year, this system may suit an isolated craft-worker, but it makes the employment of other workers and the organization of a regular industry difficult to arrange. Novelty is an important characteristic of the successful toy from the commercial point of view, and there is no necessity for the production of great numbers of toys exactly similar in size and design. Thus it is found that the agents who supply large shops are often willing to buy all the toys made by small groups of handicraft workers when the latter are able to show originality and skill in design together with good, though not necessarily elaborate, workmanship. Carved wooden toys seem to be particularly successful, and flat figures cut out with a fret-saw and painted are also in demand, whilst for soft toys the market seems to be more uncertain, although some makers have achieved success.

The Battlejack industry is an example of one which started on a small scale, on the lines of a home craft, but, producing goods which took the public fancy, has developed into a thriving concern on ordinary industrial lines, supplying through agents, the big shops of the West End of London and of other large towns. Judicious publicity achieved a great deal for this industry and the popularity of these leather caps and gloves for motoring is not likely to decline. The sales recorded in the Bloxworth sunbonnet industry in the year 1919–20 were, through shops and depots, £31 5s. 8d., through exhibitions, £80 12s. 4d., and through private orders, £61 10s. 11d. The last two methods of sale were probably closely connected, so that the exhibitions evidently provided a very much better market than the shops. The string-soled shoes made at Longleat are sold through private orders and are also bought for games or gymnasium wear in L.C.C. schools and for an institution at Brighton. Some return later to the makers to be re-soled. In 1920 over 2,000 pairs were sold and, out of an outlay of £700, £500 had been paid back by sales. The prices in 1921 varied from 4s. 2d. to 7s. 8½d., according to size, for the canvas shoes, and from 4s. 9d. to 9s. 1d. for the felt and pergamoid shoes. Babies' shoes were sold at from 3s. 7d. to 5s. 1½d. The price for re-soling was 6d. to 1s.

The difficulty of attempting to market handicraft work through the ordinary trade channels is exemplified by the experience of a woman maker of cane baskets working in an isolated village. Her work was good enough to be ordered by a well-known London shop, which would take some hundreds of waste-paper baskets at Christmas time and some fifty or so from time to time during the rest of the year. This, however, did not form the whole of her output and she found it very difficult to get into touch with other shops of the kind which would take her goods. Unless she could supply them direct to a retailer the profits of an extra middleman made the price of the baskets too high.

The Chipping Campden craftsmen, whose guild has been in existence for about thirty years, are now well known and therefore able to obtain orders. The early years of the guild in London probably helped them to get into touch with markets. Many of these craftsmen, such as the makers of stained-glass windows and the sculptors, do work which is not suitable for shop sale. These, however, are workshop industries, and not home crafts, but the guild is a part of the arts and crafts movement in its aims and organization. The silversmith's work is more easily marketable by ordinary methods, and some of it is sold in a handicrafts shop in the neighbouring village of Broadway, whilst visitors to the work-rooms occasionally buy it. The makers of jewellery and enamel ware, who used to be members of the guild and who sold this work from a shop in Campden itself, have ceased to make it, owing to the lack of any adequate outlet— a curious situation, for one would expect that these small articles could easily be sent away to other markets.

The greater part of the output of the Newton metal industry is sold from the showroom attached to the workshop. The showroom is nothing more than a shed, with no shop window, and such a place of sale, in a small, out-of-the-way village, would not seem, at first sight, to be very promising. Nevertheless, £200 worth of work was disposed of in this way during 1922. Newton is about six miles from Cambridge, whence many customers come, partly out of interest in the enterprise. The promoter is well known in the district and probably his wide circle of acquaintances helps to advertise the work. Once it has been seen its intrinsic merit will attract the customer to return. Some of the work is sold through two shops, in Leicester and Warwick, but as a rule it has been found better not to sell through shops, as people like to buy the things from the workroom if they think they cannot be obtained elsewhere. The whole stock is generally sold out at Christmas time.

Certain districts are more suitable than others for handicraft shops,[1] for example, the Lake District, which, by the beauty of its scenery, attracts tourists of aesthetic tastes and constitutes an excellent centre for the sale of this work, the ' Shakespeare country ' of Warwickshire, a ' show village ', such as Broadway, and the villages and small country towns of Sussex, all provide opportunities for a market amongst visitors and wealthy residents. Americans seem to be particularly susceptible to the appeal of quaint and original handwork. Seaside towns generally offer but a poor market, their habitués seeming to prefer the cheaper factory products, although something with a particular local association may attract them. But even in such an unlikely spot as Stroud, a little manufacturing town, a woman successfully runs a small shop for the sale of her own leather work and hand-made jewellery, and the output of other workers as well, including pictures and pottery. The prices charged are moderate, and after some years of struggle the shop is beginning to pay its way, having become known to residents in the surrounding country.

[1] See section i of this chapter, p. 79, and also Chapter II, ' Weaving ', pp. 7 et seq.

The Women's Institute shops are often established not so much with the idea of making money as of improving and keeping up the standard of the work, making it more practical, and giving the workers an added interest by supplying them with a definite aim. The organization of the shop usually depends, to a certain extent, on voluntary work. A certain amount of support is sure to be forthcoming from those interested in this widespread movement. Therefore these W. I. shops have not the same difficulties to contend against as an isolated handicraft worker or group of workers running a shop, which must yield a certain amount of profit or fail. Nevertheless, the Institute shops, which often originate as a small show of work for sale on a table in the County office or at a market town Institute 'centre', have a certain significance in the Arts and Crafts movement, and may pave the way for further enterprises on more commercial lines. The well-known Dunchurch shop in Warwickshire, which arose out of the Women's Institute glove industry there, is an excellent example, more fully developed than many of the others. It is run by a group of five Institutes in neighbouring villages, but the Dunchurch workers supply most of the stock. The shop is well situated in the centre of the village on one of the main roads from Coventry. A good many of the customers are visitors to the village, which has a good hotel much patronized by motorists ; there is also a big school in Dunchurch and parents visiting the school often call at the shop. A great many orders are received by post, both from former visitors to Dunchurch and from others who have come to know of the industry through exhibitions. Institute members take charge of the shop by turn. All goods are sold on a commission basis of 1s. 8d. in the pound, and of this 1s. goes to the seller as payment for services and 8d. towards the general expenses of upkeep. Prices are settled according to a scale, a fixed sum being paid to the workers for each kind of work, with graduations according to the quality of the workmanship. A committee of management considers all the work submitted, fixes the prices and rejects really poor work. This industry was visited in 1923, when it had been carried on for over three years and the shop had been open for over two years. £10 was borrowed from the W. I. funds with which to start business, and this has since been repaid from the profits made and a further sum of £10 contributed to W. I. funds. Thus a number of part-time workers have been enabled to obtain fair payment for as much work as they could do, provided that it came up to the standard, but obviously the profits, apart from the workers' earnings, would not have supported any one who had tried to run the shop for a livelihood.

A shop in Warwick is run on somewhat similar lines, but this provides an outlet for goods made by workers throughout the county, each Institute paying a small annual contribution towards the expenses of the shop for the privilege of sending its work there, whilst a commission of 2d. in the shilling is also charged on all work sold. In this case the workers fix the prices of their own goods. The shop is well situated in one of the main streets and most of the sales are made in the summer to visitors to the town, of whom there are a large number. £500 worth of goods was sold in the first year.

There are many different types of handicraft shop, many of them with their own special devices to attract customers. There is a delightful one at Broadway, where a picturesque old house and a collection of antiques provide a good setting for the hand-woven furnishing materials from the loom of a local weaver, the elm furniture also made in the village, wrought iron trivets and candlesticks from the Chipping Campden workshops, leather and raffia work, baskets, and other articles from different workers. The things are arranged as they might be in a home. Prices are high but seem to suit the purses of the wealthy tourists who call at the village.

There are a number of shops or depots, not always as well arranged as this one, where nothing is made on the spot, but where the output of many workers is sold, usually on a commission basis. A more interesting type of shop is that run by a group of craftsmen or a guild. The shops of the Artificers' Guild are an example, and, on a humbler scale, there are many small shops throughout the country carried on by groups of workers in several crafts. A weaving room or some other workshop on the premises is often an additional attraction to visitors, and customers who are really interested in crafts like to discuss the work with the makers and are able to give special orders and arrange to have any piece of work designed to meet their taste. This is probably the kind of handicraft shop which can be most easily worked up from a small beginning, particularly in places where there is a ' summer season ' for visitors, with little opportunity for sales in the winter, when most of the work can be done. The handicraft shop which only sells other people's work on commission may be handicapped by the fact that the workers in the neighbourhood also sell

their work at wholesale prices to chance visitors to their
work-rooms. This should be prevented by a proper agreement between maker and retailer, and in some cases there
is an understanding to the effect that the retailer has the
copyright of certain designs, which the maker will not sell
elsewhere.

Where goods are sold on commission the amount charged
may be anything between 5 per cent. and 45 per cent.,
accordingly to the lines on which the selling organization
is conducted. Local Arts and Crafts exhibitions, which are
organized mainly by the workers themselves, may charge
only 5 per cent. commission, but stall space must also be
rented, and the gate money helps to pay expenses. The
Home Arts and Industries Association charges 10 per cent.,
again with a charge for space to the exhibitors, finding that
this is the least amount which will serve to cover overhead
expenses. In the Longleat shoe industry the prices are
based on an 8 per cent. profit, but in this case there is no
shop, the shoes being sold to local people or else through
the post. The manager of the industry gives her work
voluntarily. In the numerous depots for the sale of handicraft work which exist in the south-west of England, the
commission was found to be usually from 10 per cent. to
25 per cent., which is a small amount if the shop is being
run for profit. The commission at the Women's Institute
shop in Winchester is 2d. in the shilling, or 16⅔ per cent.,
and in the Warwick shop the charge is the same, as it also
seems frequently to be at the W. I. exhibitions. The
Dunchurch shop is carried on by means of only a penny in
the shilling, or 8⅓ per cent. commission, but the profit made
is very small. The Newton metal industry takes 20 per cent.
for expenses, no profit being made, but in this case a workshop and tools are provided. 33⅓ per cent. is the usual
amount of commission charged by shops which are run for
profit, in the case of small organizations in the country, but
for larger shops in towns 50 per cent. is not unusual. The
Newlyn metal work is sold by agents in the seaside towns on
a 25 per cent. commission basis.

v. *Some Difficulties.*

Generally speaking, the organizations for the development
of home crafts aim either at the revival or preservation of
ancient craft-skill, or they encourage the teaching of crafts
to village people for the sake of their educational value and

the interest which they arouse in the workers, or, again, the chief object of the promoters may be to provide the rural population with an additional source of income and a means of turning to account their spare time in the slack seasons of agriculture.   There are also individuals who carry on a handicraft industry for their own livelihood, but who often become interested in the general Arts and Crafts movement in its relation to village life and take part in it by teaching craft classes or by training apprentices.   Any organization may combine the three aims, but as a rule one or another of them provides the leading motive, and the nature of the organization may vary in accordance with it.

The decline of the system of giving out work from factories to be done in the workers' homes [1] may increase the need in certain districts for other means of earning money by home work.   Although the factory out-work is often of great value to the women who rely on it to add to the family income, yet the system has many drawbacks.   The work is nearly always very poorly paid, and usually only takes firm root in a poor industrial neighbourhood or in a rural district where the condition of the agricultural labouring-classes is bad.   The existence of out-work, once it is established, will help to keep the general wages of the district on a low level, because there is this additional means of livelihood by which other members of the family may eke out the income of the chief wage-earner.   The extensive development of the home crafts movement might tend towards the same evil effects as have resulted from the out-work system unless the organizers of the movement have some knowledge of economics and of the social history of rural areas, and bear in mind the dangers which are to be avoided.

The Women's Institute movement lays stress on the educational value of home crafts and does not include the carrying on of industries, as such, in the main lines of its organization.   In addition to the teaching of crafts which may become the groundwork of industries, the Women's Institutes hold classes in many crafts which the workers will only practise for their own use, such as dress-making and ' household jobbery '.

The Home Arts and Industries Association is also a body whose primary aim is educational, although the classes started under its auspices may develop into self-supporting industries and remain affiliated to the association.

[1] See vol. ii, *Osier Growing, Basketry Industries and Some Rural Factories,* Part II, Chapter III, ' Outwork for Factories '.

Many difficulties must be overcome by the organizers of home crafts. The organization of scattered workers is a problem which usually has to be dealt with in the early stages of an industry. The systems commonly in force in the case of out-workers for a factory and in the lace-making industry may be useful as models. The factory procedure is that an employee, who may herself work at the trade, should be responsible for distributing, collecting, and overlooking the work and that the payments should pass through her hands. She is paid either a weekly sum or a commission on her work. Pillow-lace in the counties of Buckingham and Bedford is often collected by dealers who travel from village to village, buying up the lace and supplying the workers with cotton and with new patterns.[1]

The dependence of a village industry on its voluntary organizers often causes a further difficulty when these leave the district or give up the work for other reasons, for they are not easy to replace, and the better they have worked the greater is this difficulty. In such an organizer, keen personal interest in the workers must be combined with the willingness and capacity to teach, to keep accounts, to visit and to carry on a considerable amount of correspondence. Therefore, although voluntary work may provide the foundation from which a successful home industry is built up, it is a wise provision to employ paid helpers as the work develops and funds are available, or else to bring the work into line with that of some official body in the county which may assist with the organization. The Rural Community Councils which have recently been formed in several counties, and which have as one of their aims the encouragement of rural industries, may be of assistance in this direction, especially in the co-ordination of individual enterprises.

Another difficulty which has already been referred to is the irregularity of the output of spare-time home-workers, which makes the execution of orders uncertain. In many cases it has been found, as in the Newton metal industry, that a few regular full-time workers provide a good basis for an industry, and if they can be found and can be assured of adequate wages, the enterprise will benefit considerably by being able to count upon an assured output of a known standard. Even if no full-time workers can be obtained, a few who can guarantee to give a certain number of hours weekly will be of great value. When the foundation of a steady output has thus been laid, orders can be obtained

[1] See Chapter III, ' Lace-making '.

which will provide a stimulus for all the workers and keep up their interest in co-operation and good craftsmanship.

The failure to relate the work taken up to local conditions, to consider local supplies of raw material or local opportunities for marketing goods, have already been dealt with. Craftswomen have taken up rush-work, buying the rushes from importers or dealers, without exploring the possibilities of cutting rushes which grow in the district. Wooden bowls and other articles are bought at a high price from some firm which supplies craft-work materials, when a local village turner could make these things more cheaply and would often be glad of the work. Or, again, village women are taught to do decorative leather-work of the more elaborate and expensive kind, for which they have no opportunity of finding a market. Such mistakes as these characterize some of the less well-organized enterprises, but in other cases local resources are used to the fullest extent.

The wages problem has been dealt with fully above. It is impossible to fix a universal rate, because local methods of organization, standards of skill, and marketing facilities differ so widely, but there seems to be need for fuller information on the subject and for co-operation and agreement as to certain standards.

A difficulty which is often found in Women's Institutes when it is proposed to organize an industry, is the lack of concentration. The women are often keener on having demonstrations of different crafts, and on gaining by this means a smattering of knowledge about them, than in taking courses of craft classes, or, even when a course is arranged, the workers may prove anxious to hurry on to a new craft before they have practised the one already learnt. It is true that the aim of Women's Institutes is to brighten the lives of village women rather than to organize industries, but probably the ability to practise one handicraft really well would have a more lasting brightening influence on a woman's life than the hazy idea, gathered from demonstrations, of how several handicrafts are done.

The prospects of individual industries are often difficult to estimate, because the collapse of any one of them may be due either to the fact that there is not a good enough market for the work, to some weakness in the organization, or to a failure to get into touch with the market. Many which enjoyed a temporary prosperity during the war have flagged since, but others seem to show considerable possibilities for further development. The Longleat shoe industry, for example, was beginning to flag in 1921 owing to the number of cheap factory-made slippers which were being put on the market, but if it failed as an industry there might be a useful life ahead of it as a craft for home use. Cane basket-making and the dyeing of cane and raffia have as yet been little exploited as home-craft industries, but it seems likely there are openings for further developments, particularly in the dyeing of these materials in good colours for sale in small quantities to other handicraft workers. The fur-craft industry in Herefordshire had already shown in 1921 that beautiful work of this kind could be done and that there was a ready sale for the output, although it was only a small one. There is also a sale for the undressed skins, which are merely dried in much the same way as the moleskins are treated and sold thus to trade furriers for dressing and making up. A fur-craft industry which breeds its own supply of rabbits, specializing in the kinds with the more beautiful furs, should not be difficult to start in a village. Perhaps the greatest obstacle is the seasonal nature of the work, for it is only during a few weeks of the year, usually in December, that the skins are of any use for fur work. Once the skins are dressed, however, they can, of course, be made up at any time, and now, when a large proportion of all the furs generally worn have their origin on the back of the humble rabbit, there should be a ready sale for any surplus of cured skins which the industry could not deal with further.

In considering the possibilities for the development of handicraft industries, it must be remembered that the importance of originality of design and of individual craftsmanship makes it advisable to restrict the size of these industries, although this should not prevent a certain amount of co-operation between the small enterprises, especially for the purposes of obtaining raw materials and of marketing the output. One of the Chipping Campden craftsmen declared that the character of the work could not be preserved at its best with a staff of more than four workers. The number would vary according to the nature of the craft and the method of organization, but probably should seldom exceed a dozen. As regards the desirability of the development of home-work, the opinion of a Trade Union leader of gloveresses is interesting. ' What I should like to see ', she said, ' is a development of *beautiful* work. We don't want the homes turned into factories. Factory-work is soul-destroying and the country people have more soul than those in the towns.' This is particularly significant as coming from a representative of industrial rather than craft work.

Attention has already been drawn to the fact that the desirability of developing certain home industries is very doubtful. Lace-making has always been a sweated industry and although many enthusiasts may be led to ignore this fact, carried away by the antiquarian interest and the beauty of the work, yet it seems unlikely that it can ever be really well paid.

In the case of basket-making there is the danger of injuring the business of the ordinary small country makers, and the situation is further complicated by the presence of so many blinded and disabled men in this trade. The position of the regular industry is dealt with in another volume,[1] and it is clearly shown that there is at present no room for new workers in willow, although, as far as cane is concerned, there is more chance of breaking fresh ground. The blind craftsmen already have difficulty in finding a market for their work, not because it is inferior in quality, but because in this, as in other crafts, they are unable to compete in speed with the sighted workers. They can only make certain types of baskets, but their craftsmanship is excellent and they receive the most careful training. It is true that the number of baskets made by independent craft-workers and those of the Women's Institutes is small, but it seems to be increasing. It was stated in one county that basketry is one of the things most easily disposed of in the Institute handicraft shop and at the sales of work, and many Institute members in the county were enthusiastic as to the quality of the work produced and the prospect for further development of the industry. It seems that the workers are so readily able to dispose of these baskets, because, on the one hand they work in their spare time and so are content with a low rate of earnings insufficient for the regular maker, and because, on the other hand, many of the purchasers intend to buy some of the Institute work from motives of interest and sympathy, and a basket being comparatively cheap, portable, and useful, is chosen in preference to a rush-mat or a piece of embroidery. Thus it may be unlikely that the willow basket-making industry amongst Women's Institute members will increase to a sufficient extent to interfere radically with the whole English industry, beyond the possible diversion of a few orders from

[1] See vol. ii, *Osier Growing, Basketry Industries and Some Rural Factories.*

the local basket-maker or Institute for the Blind. Nevertheless, a course which involves even the possibility of this is, under present economic conditions, one to be avoided, particularly by an organization which aims at helping working-class people to improve their conditions of life and at promoting friendly relations between all classes of the community.

Amongst the most important factors on which will depend the future success of handicrafts industries, good and thorough teaching and a high standard constantly set before the workers, may perhaps rank as the first. Business-like organization of the industry, fair payment of workers, a method of sale which does not involve too heavy overhead expenses, are all necessary. But even if all these elements of success are present no industry will have a real and independent life without the spirit of true craftsmanship ; patronage will not keep it alive when the patrons have turned their attention elsewhere. A business-like organization may lead to the development of an industry on factory lines but will not, by itself, produce good craft-work. Only the workers' love of and interest in their work, which is the outcome of skill acquired by patience and steady concentration, will make of the industry not only a means of earning money —valuable as that may be to village men and women—but also a real part of their lives and a method of self-expression.

CHAPTER V

RURAL POTTERIES

i. *Location*.

POTTERIES of old standing are always found near beds of local clay, for the difficulty of transporting such a heavy and bulky material determined their site. In addition to the clay the other great need of the potter is fuel for the kiln, and until modern times it was more economical to burn thousands of faggots from neighbouring woods than to settle near a coal deposit and attempt to transport the clay. The potteries of Devonshire have a longer history than any others in England. At Barnstaple the potter's art claims an unbroken tradition of fifteen hundred years [1] and the name ' Barum ware ' for pottery produced at Barnstaple is of a remote date. Anti-quarians believe that the industry has been carried on continuously from Roman times. The clay beds around Barnstaple have certainly provided raw material for the industry for many hundreds of years, and in the ancient records of the town there are numerous allusions to the potteries. The modern Cross Street was in the fourteenth century ' Crock Street ', where pottery was sold, and there is still a ' Potter's Lane ' and a part of the town called Pottingdon. Harvest jugs were one of the staple products of Barnstaple and one of the favourite mottoes engraved upon them ran :

Fill me full of liquor sweet
For that is good when friends do meet ;
When friends do meet and liquor 's plenty,
Fill me again when I be empty.

It was one which the potters themselves, according to tradi-tion, obeyed. ' Long Tom ', ' Ferret Tail ', ' Gully Mouth ', ' Punch Gut ', ' Sixties ', and ' Penny Joog ' are the familiar descriptions, in their relative order according to size, of the pitchers from largest to smallest. They were sold by the ' tale ', or by the ' land dozen ', which was thirty-nine, or the ' sea dozen ', which was sixty.

[1] Papers read to the Devonshire Society in 1881 and 1891. Vol. xiii, *The Potter's Art in Devonshire*, J. Phillips ; vol. xxiii, *The Potteries of North Devon*, H. W. Strong.

Bideford also had potteries in the fourteenth century ; church tiles were made here and clay ovens which were sent to Bude. Vessels known as ' fish stains ', in which pilchards were pickled, were another Bideford product, the three sizes being known, according to measure, as ' great crocks ', ' buzzards ', and ' gallons '. Oil lamps made of pottery were a common article of manufacture at Bideford for many years, and old people can remember them as being the only lights burned in all the houses of the surrounding country as late as 1880.

In spite of the problem of fuel—so much more pressing to a potter to-day than in the early days of the industry— many potteries are still to be found of which the site is entirely due to local beds of clay. In nearly every case such potteries have remained small—compared with the big industrialized factories of Staffordshire—for the potteries that are intended either to turn out goods in great quantities or to manufacture a very elaborate article find it more economical to be situated near coal fields and to bring their clay by rail or sea. In the case of mass production very little hand-work is done and the industry needs a large number of unskilled workers and a highly specialized industrial organization, as well as a high capitalization on account of the expensive machinery used. In the manufacture of delicate china a large variety of constituent elements is required from different sources—some from abroad—and a greater bulk of coal than of clay is used. The output of the rural potteries, therefore, is of a simple kind and usually of a type which depends upon a certain amount of hand-work either for decorative or utilitarian reasons. Except for a few very small enterprises carried on by artists, the rural potteries are to be found on beds of clay from which they obtain the bulk of the raw material used.

In nearly all the potteries of Dorset and Devon local potters' clay forms the ' body ', generally unmixed, for some of the finest and best potters' clay is found in these districts. The china clay, which is found chiefly in Cornwall and of which great quantities are sent to Staffordshire and abroad, is of a different kind. The Teign Valley is rich in white clay, and this is used in local potteries both for ' body ' and for decoration. At Kingsteignton iron-stained clay is used locally at a big pottery where drain-pipes are made. Up the valley towards Bovey Tracey there are several beds and mines, and at Bovey itself is a big pottery where white household ware is made from local clay. At Watcombe, close to

K 2

Torquay, there are good beds of red clay, and also at Aller Vale, near Newton Abbot. Both these deposits are used in potteries on the spot, where so-called ' art goods ' are made. The ' body ' is generally of red clay, the white clay from Kingsteignton near by being used for decoration. The pottery so made is called Aller Vale ware. At Fremingham, near Barnstaple, there are rich beds of a darker clay used for the ' body ' of the Barum ware. Besides two potteries at Barnstaple itself there is a small one at Braunton, five miles away.

In Dorset white clay is worked around Poole Harbour and somewhat to the west of it, and blue clay at Wareham, near Poole. An encaustic tile works at Poole also produces hand-thrown table pottery which has won a name for unique and beautiful work of good form and decoration and delicate colouring. At Truro (Cornwall) there is an old-fashioned pottery which makes bread pans, pitchers, bowls, and other large household ware for sale in the surrounding countryside. There is a firm at Verwood, in the New Forest, run on similar lines, using the local clay which is very compact in substance and which burns a pleasing buff colour. A pottery at Poole was using Verwood clay for ornamenting the scented ware which was in vogue in 1921 when these potteries were visited, and which was made also at Crediton, Bovey Tracey, and Honiton (where a deserted kiln had been brought into use again for this purpose). Many ' crocks ' used to be produced at the tile works at Gillingham in Dorset. In Cornwall an enterprise which may have a very interesting future had, when the district was visited, lately been started at St. Ives. An artist who has spent many years studying the potter's art in China and Japan had built a kiln here and was experimenting in Japanese methods.

There are several rural potteries in Sussex. One of the oldest of these is at Rye, where the making of bricks, drainpipes, tiles, and flower-pots from a local bed of ' terra-cotta ' [1] was started about three generations ago. By 1922, however, little of the local clay was used, supplies being obtained from Devon and Dorset. At Deal a pottery has been running for twenty years. The discovery of a bed of clay here, the usual ' terra-cotta ' found in the south-eastern counties, was made by a Staffordshire potter on a holiday. Whilst visiting Deal Castle he was struck by the quality of the bricks used in its construction. He saw that the clay of which they were made must have been of a much finer quality than that

[1] The term is used by the potters to describe, not the finished pottery, but the clay from which it is made.

usually employed for this purpose, and realizing that in all likelihood it was from a local bed he set himself to discover it. Eventually he found it and has worked it ever since. This pottery makes a few bricks and many flower-pots and tiles as well as the vases and other decorative work in which the manager is chiefly interested.

The Potters' Art Guild at Compton, three miles from Guildford, which was founded twenty years ago by the painter, G. F. Watts, uses the red clay of the district for garden jars, bird baths, feeding tables for birds, sundials, memorial tablets, garden statuettes, and fountains. A great deal of grey clay from Dorset and Devon is also used, but it is found that for things which must stand weather, particularly for the memorial tablets and railings round graves which are intended to last for a long time, the local ' terracotta ' is more durable. Pottery made from the grey clays shows signs of wear after twenty years. Where colour is to be added, as in the ' biscuit ' vases and the medallions which are also produced here, grey clay must be used, for terracotta does not take colour well. It has, however, a very beautiful colour of its own and the result when it is used by itself is pleasing. Actually, more of the many-coloured wares than of garden ornaments, for which terra-cotta is more suitable, are made, and so a greater quantity of the grey clay is used. In fact this pottery was not started on account of the presence of clay in the neighbourhood, but was founded by G. F. Watts and his wife in the village in which they happened to live. The terra-cotta garden work can be produced at a relatively low cost, whereas it would be expensive if the great quantity of clay used in the making of these large articles had to be brought from a distance. The statuettes, for example, for garden pedestals are sold for about £2 2s. each for copies, although an original design may cost £10.

There are many firms in the south-eastern counties producing primarily bricks and tiles but sometimes a few other things as well, for example, at Burgess Hill, Chailey and Uckfield, Sevenoaks and Tonbridge, and Ditchling Common. At the last place mouldings for doorways and bas reliefs are made. Moulded pottery ornaments—models of Canterbury Cathedral, the pilgrim's water-bottle, various crosses, and so on—are made by two women in Canterbury from local clay mixed with some from Faversham. Farmers in the Sussex Weald are said to make ' clamp bricks ' of clay from their own fields without the use of a kiln.

The best work of this district is that produced at Lower Dicker, near Hailsham—the well-known and beautiful Dicker ware. It is made from the ordinary wealden clay, the same as that which is largely used for bricks and tiles. A peculiar dull black glaze is the one most usually associated with this ware, but other glazes also are used, in particular an amber one, splashed on the pot and looking as if it had been spilled over the edge. The same firm makes bread crocks, fireproof cooking and other pottery, all from the local clay. There have been pottery works here since 1843, but it is only during the last ten years that the distinctive glazes now associated with Dicker ware have been made.

Apart from the important potteries of the south-western counties and the two or three of the south-eastern there are not many small rural potteries. At Weatheriggs, near Penrith, brown earthenware for kitchen use is made. The bed of clay has been dug for many years and is not at all large. Deep basins for kneading bread in are among the articles produced, and also ' bread mugs '— large, deep jars about two feet high in which bread is kept. The works are on a very small scale and only kiln once a fortnight. There is a pottery at Burton-in-Lonsdale, on the borders of Yorkshire and Lancashire, which has been established for over a hundred years. Two men are employed to mine the clay from under an adjoining hill-side, whence it is brought out by a truck on a light railway running into the tunnel under the hill. There is also a seam of coal a few inches in depth found alongside the clay and this is brought out and used to some extent in the engine. Only spirit jars were being made when the pottery was visited, but there was some idea of utilizing other local clays for the flower-pots, cream jugs, milk basins, &c. which were made until a few years ago by other firms in the neighbourhood. Although coal is mined at Ingleton, near by, it is not of a quality good enough for the kilns, and the greater part of the fuel used comes to this isolated spot from Leeds and Normanton.

In spite of the fact that flower-pots are things which are needed in great quantities all of uniform pattern, they are one of the few kinds of pottery in common use which can only be made by the method of hand-throwing. Twenty years ago experiments were made in producing them by machinery, but it was found that the clay became too densely welded, so that the pots were not sufficiently porous and plants would not live in them. There are therefore a few rural potteries, generally of old standing and often run on primitive lines,

which produce them. One at Diss, near Wattisfield in
Suffolk, also makes pots of other kinds. There is said to be
enough clay here to last another fifty years. Some of the
Sussex firms already mentioned also make flower-pots. In
Essex, four miles from Waltham Cross, on the borders of
Epping Forest, there is a pottery nearly a hundred years
old which turns out flower-pots and a few chimney-pots and
drain-pipes, and there are two similar firms not far away, at
Tottenham, on the borders of London and Middlesex, in
a district which is now the opposite of rural. Others are at
Woodside, near Leicester, at Sheffield, and at Weston-super-
Mare, and until four years ago flower-pots were made at
brick works near Northampton.

A few small potteries were heard of which had recently
been closed. At Cranham, in Gloucestershire, there were
until twelve years ago two potteries in the woods, making
rough brown kitchen-ware—crocks, jugs, and pitchers—
from local clay. At Stamford, in Lincolnshire, terra-cotta
ware was formerly made where there is now only a brick and
tile works. A small pottery works in Bishop Auckland
(Durham), which was closed down in 1913, seems to have
been similar in character to some of the rural industries,
although the district is an industrial one and proximity to
the coal fields seems to have been the main factor in deciding
the situation, a small seam of brick clay providing the raw
material. Earthenware and fire-clay ware were made on
a small scale and also brown ware—big bowls in which milk
stands for the cream to rise, and others bigger than these for
the miners' wives to bake their pies in. Other typical products were the huge fire-proof basins in which bread was
baked—known as ' punks ' in Durham, ' joles ' in Staffordshire, and ' bowles ' (rhyming with fowls) in Yorkshire.

There are one or two potteries still in existence in industrial
areas which are interesting because they retain much of the
character of rural industries, although it is probable that
before long they will either die out or be developed on
industrial lines. One of these is situated, appropriately
enough, in a suburb of Sunderland known by the rural name
of Sheepfolds. It was started in 1848 by one man with about
three workers. The clay was quarried on the spot—the
river bank—and the present works are built in the old
quarries, having been extended as the clay was dug out.
Quarrying has now come to an end, having reached the road
and buildings, but since the whole of Sunderland stands
on a bed of clay, raw material can be obtained from any

excavations made in the city when new buildings are put up. Probably the adjacent coal-fields originally determined the site of this pottery, but all the fuel now used comes from Newcastle, the local coal not being suitable. Brown ware for household use is made here, and there is a similar firm at Millfields, another suburb of Sunderland.

Another industrial pottery which is of interest from the point of view of small industries is the Ruskin factory at Smethwick, near Birmingham. Some of its glazes need firing at a high temperature and ware of this sort cannot be made economically in rural districts, but its exceedingly small scale and the fact that all the ware is made by hand brings it near to the country potteries in organization and interest.

ii. *The Clay and its Treatment.*

Many of the great clay beds of Devonshire are underground, whence the clay is dug out by miners, as it is at Burton-in-Lonsdale. At Kingsteignton seventy men are employed in the mines. At Bovey Tracey the clay is worked both in quarries and underground. As it comes up from the mine the clay in Devonshire is sorted and then sold for the different purposes for which each kind is suitable. The quality of clay differs very much and the output of any pottery dependent on local supplies must be planned accordingly. For example, the small pottery at Wattisfield sorts the clay found and used there into three grades. The kind known as ' best earth ' is used for meat pots, ' next quality ' makes flower-pots, and ' third quality ' is only good enough for bricks. This firm has occasionally used Cornish white clay but it employs chiefly the local red. This is very good but rather deep, and sometimes has a great deal of iron in it. Although this does not affect the actual quality of the clay for utilitarian purposes, it spoils its appearance, giving it a curious dark metallic look which makes it unsuitable for meat pots, in which a nice appearance is necessary. For flower-pots, in which the colour is not of importance, this clay is excellent.

The preparation of clay is very important, in order to get good results in the firing. It must be smooth for the thrower to work and of the same consistency throughout. In the larger potteries of the south-western counties machinery is used for preparing the clay in bulk. The same engines work the wheels and lathes and other appliances. If the clay is good, small quantities can be dealt with by hand. Richard

CLAY AND ITS TREATMENT 137

Lunn, in his book on pottery, points out that it can be made from the clay from any brickyard, 'provided this is first made into " slip ", the name given to it when mixed with water to a smooth and creamy consistency and then passed through a sieve of phosphor gauze '.[1] The following method is used in some of the large Devonshire potteries. The clay is dug from the site, heaped up to weather during the winter so that the frost shall make it more friable, churned up with water by machinery, shaken by hand through silk gauze and conducted by machinery to a press where the water is squeezed out, leaving it stiff enough to be shaped into balls and thrown on the wheel. At Crediton the thrower's assistant was seen to take up the clay in both hands and fling it down on to a board many times till it was of the right consistency and moisture for the thrower. The state of moisture needed depends upon the use to which it is to be put. For big and heavy pots it must be stiffer than for small pieces, to prevent them from sagging with their own weight before they are dry enough for firing. Big pots therefore mean harder work for the thrower, as the clay is stiffer to manipulate.

Most of the potteries in the south-western counties prepare the clay in their own works, but a few of the smaller ones prefer to obtain it, ready for use, from bigger firms. The system adopted depends upon the amount of preparation needed for the particular material. Verwood clay, for instance, needs only to be put through a press, if it has sand mixed in with it, in order to take out the grittiness. This clay is not only used in the local potteries but is sold to others. In order to cheapen production for the popular scented ware, one pottery used a different method of preparing the clay. Instead of being made into slip it was merely put through a pugging mill, worked by a horse, which crushed the grit to powder. This method supplied six throwers with clay for a week at a labour cost of only 10s., whereas £10 spent on ' slipping ' clay would only provide two men with material for a few days' work. The result of the cheaper process was good enough for the cheap ornaments made by this firm, but the method is not reliable and depends on the quality of the clay, whilst roughness in the material supplied to the thrower makes his work more difficult.

In a few potteries the preliminary preparation of the clay —the grinding and mixing—is still carried out by means of a very primitive pugging mill, turned by a horse, as at Verwood, Wattisfield, and Fakenham. In the pottery at

[1] Richard Lunn, *Pottery*. Chapman and Hall.

Sheepfolds electric motors have recently been installed to replace a gas engine for working both the pugging mill for grinding the clay and also the wheels. At Burton-in-Lonsdale the engine now used to turn the three potters' wheels and the wheel used for ' jollying ' and to work the pugging machine is practically the only innovation since the pottery was started a hundred years ago. Most of the Devon potteries have engines for this work. The foot lever by means of which the thrower regulates the speed of the power-driven wheel is more easily controlled than was the boy who formerly turned it. Considerable saving in labour is also effected. In one pottery the use of the engine which works ten potters' wheels and a number of lathes was said to save £15 a week in labour at a cost of £1 in fuel.

iii. *The Craftsmen and their Work.*

The chief artist and craftsman of the typical small rural pottery is the thrower, who moulds the clay on his wheel into the form which it is, by its nature, fitted to take. The ' body ', prepared from local clay, is in many cases hardly any finer than that used for flower-pots or bricks. The pots which are made must be adapted to the potentialities of the material, that is, they must be somewhat thick and bold of form ; the thrower's problem is to get them light enough without sacrificing strength. The potter may modify his material by mixing it with clays imported from other districts, but the fewer ' foreign ' ingredients he uses, the greater the economy. In the large factories of the industrial districts the basis of the potter's art is quite different ; here the chemist in his laboratory is the master craftsman and upon his skill in devising ' bodies ' of compounded clays, suitable to the different kinds of ware to be made, depends much of the success of the industry.

It is the process of hand-throwing, therefore, that gives distinctive character to the ware produced by the small rural pottery. Some of the rural firms, however, have introduced the mechanical processes—typical of the factory industry—of lathe-turning and ' jollying '. In some cases inexperienced or unskilful throwers are employed to throw a rough shape which is fined down on a lathe, but the character of a hand-thrown pot is thus lost and, so far as appearance goes, the first shaping might as well have been done by a machine. The preliminary hand-throwing serves, however, to give the pot the durability of hand-welded ware

MIXING THE CLAY.   A PRIMITIVE METHOD

MOULDING

POTTERY

and is thus useful in the case of the spirit jars made at Burton-in-Lonsdale, where the largest—holding from four to six gallons—are ' made rough ' by the hand-thrower and finished by ' jollying '. If mechanical processes are used to such an extent that the advantages of hand-thrown ware are lost entirely the rural pottery may be brought into disastrous competition with the big factories of Staffordshire.

Each thrower has an assistant who shapes the required quantity of clay into a ball. In some potteries the clay is weighed to ensure uniformity in the bulk of every pot. The ball of clay is passed to the thrower, who tosses it into the centre of the potter's wheel—a revolving disk—raising and pressing it down again as the wheel turns, and gradually shaping it with his hands. Sometimes he has one or two gauges—pieces of metal fixed so as to give, by their height above the surface of the wheel and the distance of their points from the centre, the exact height and width of the pot. But in watching many a thrower at his wheel one is struck by his skill in shaping the pot with only his hand and his eye to guide him. The pace of the wheel must be varied to accord with the potter's work. It is sometimes turned by means of a large fly-wheel revolved by a girl or boy, who watches the potter and changes the pace to his order, sometimes by a treadle worked by the thrower himself, sometimes by mechanical power.

Large heavy vessels are the most difficult to throw. In making the Yorkshire ' punks ', for example, exact judgement is required on the part of the thrower to make the pot as thin as possible and yet strong enough, and skill and care are needed to lift the immense vessel off the wheel without causing it to fall apart.

In the jollying process clay may be spread on to a mould which gives the inner contour of a saucer or bowl ; the mould is placed on a wheel, and a metal instrument pressed down upon it gives the outer contour. Another method, employed for making pudding basins, is to start with a lump of clay in the bottom of a *hollow* mould, working the clay with the hands to spread it up the sides of the mould as the wheel revolves, and then using a metal gauge to give the inner contour. This method does not give either the characteristic ' hand-thrown ' appearance or the superior strength of the ware which is moulded by the potter's sensitive hands.

When the pots have been shaped from the clay they must be stacked away to dry for a short time, after which they are ready for the next process, that of firing—or baking—in the kiln. To fire pottery correctly needs as much skill, of another kind—calculation and nice judgement—as to throw it well and truly, and the firing has just as important an effect upon the quality of the finished ware.

The size and output of a pottery are to some extent governed by the capacity of the kiln, but this may be fired at more or less frequent intervals according to the output. The small pottery near Penrith kilns only once a fortnight. At Burton-in-Lonsdale the three kilns are all fired each week, taking three days to fire and two to cool. Twenty tons of coal are used here weekly. At Wattisfield the kiln burns from Tuesday night to Saturday morning and uses from two to three tons of coal besides thirty faggots which are put in towards the end. The coal has to come from Nottingham. At Waltham Abbey there are two big furnaces and one small one ; each of the large ones is lighted once a week, burns for three days and cools for two days. Thousands of flower-pots are baked at one firing in each of the big kilns. Four tons of coal are used each time, the coal being carted four miles from Waltham Cross station. The large kilns here are fitted inside, except for an alley from the entrance and a central space, with shelves made of pottery on which the pots are piled. The shelves last about a year and remain in place until they have to be renewed, only those in the centre having to be removed after each firing. The heat passes up flues at the sides of the furnaces, which are open at the top. Round the tops of the larger furnaces are built big attics with unglazed windows, where the pots are stacked to dry before firing. The fumes which rise from the furnace pass away through the window openings, but they are enough to make the place unhealthy to work in. The men only remain here a short time, stacking the pots which they bring up.

The kiln is brought gradually to the desired heat and then allowed to cool before the pots are taken out. Accidents in firing are not uncommon and the risk must be taken into account when estimating costs. There are nearly always some faulty pieces which must be sold as ' seconds ', and the whole kiln may be wrong. The temperature differs according to the kind of ware to be fired. It needs skill and experience to fire a kiln, and the stoker has to know his kiln as a cook must know her oven. It also requires skill to pack a kiln so that no space, and therefore no fuel, is wasted. In the first firing the pots can be put to touch one another but in the second—called in Devonshire ' firing a glost kiln '—they must be arranged so that each one is separate or the glaze would stick them together as it melts. They are piled up with ' stilts '—tiny crockery tripods—placed between each layer, the whole packed in ' saggars '—very large vessels also made of coarse pottery. These are usually bought from Staffordshire, but a few of the Devon potteries make their own. Broken crocks are one of the ingredients in a saggar. When big pots are fired, as at Verwood, no saggars are used, the pots being built above one another. A few already fired are used as steps for the man as he packs the kiln, which he enters from above. An old-fashioned way of packing was to put furze above each layer of pots and then slabs of clay ; by the time the furze is burnt away the slabs are fired and serve as platforms for the pots resting on them.

Pottery kilns in the south-western counties are fired with furze, wood, coal, or gas, and the kilns vary enormously in capacity and shape. One potter, who has a circular kiln, uses three-sided saggars with rounded corners, so as to fit his kiln compactly ; these are made in the works. Some kilns, through bad planning of the flues or other faults in construction, require more fuel in proportion to their capacity than others. Kiln building is a specialized industry, but even with a good kiln the firing needs to be planned in the light of scientific knowledge and considerable experience. The waste of fuel entailed in old-fashioned kilns unscientifically built may have accounted for the failure of some of the older potteries.

The fuel used most commonly for firing kilns is coal, but gas gives more certain results. The Truro pottery is fired with furze on the top of a little coal. ' Liquid fire '—namely flame—blazes to the top of the kiln and several feet above at the end of the firing. This is a primitive way of bringing the upper part of the kiln to a temperature as high as the lower. At Verwood the kiln is fired with wood, and a brick kiln on an estate in Norfolk uses nothing but faggots. A considerable saving of coal is effected in some kilns by what is called the circular process of firing. The top of the kiln is closed and there are chimneys up the sides within the kiln. The heat passes up through them to the roof, percolates down amongst the ware and out through a flue at the bottom. Such an arrangement is said to be an enormous saving of fuel as compared with the old method of letting the heat rise up through the kiln and pass out at the top.

In packing the kiln for firing, space is economized by using for big ware, instead of saggars, small rimmed pieces of fire-brick shaped like the segment of a circle. Three of these being placed on the rim of one bowl support another bowl or pan inside it. Stacks of bowls can thus be fitted inside one another. The fire-brick is a good conductor and the kiln can be heated to a higher temperature than would be safe if the bowls supported one another.

Pottery is baked either once or twice, according to its nature and the use to which it is to be put. Flower-pots, for example, are baked only once, in fact the porous nature of once-baked ware is in this case an essential quality of the finished article. Certain kinds of household crocks can also be finished in a single firing. Of this type are the bread pans and pitchers made at Verwood and Truro. These, if glazed at all, are only glazed inside, or else round the rim by way of decoration. Most glazed ware, however, is coated with glaze after the first firing and then fired again. In this second firing the glaze melts and is fused with the body of the pot. Since the firing of a kiln is an expensive process, ware which is only once fired can be produced at a comparatively low cost.

The scented ware which was being produced in considerable quantities in some of the Dorset potteries in 1921 was baked only once and not glazed. The vases were therefore porous and quite useless for holding water. Some were decorated with 'slip', others with oil-paint or transfers, and handles of plaited raffia were added. These ornaments could be produced very cheaply. The shapes were of a kind which a boy could quickly learn to throw and the single firing was a great economy. The ware achieved popularity not because of its hand-thrown character, nor, indeed, on account of any artistic merit, but because it was inexpensive and novel.

The Potters' Art Guild at Compton sells much of its output in the form of once-baked, or 'biscuit', ware, simply decorated with a colour wash and not baked a second time after the colouring. The rough surface of biscuit ware takes colour well and the effect is somewhat like that of a distempered wall. Bright colours are used, chiefly oranges and blues, and the vases made are attractive in appearance and cheap owing to the simplicity of the process. They are porous, however, and the colours run when they are washed. A little enamel paint on the bottom will render some of the vases sufficiently water-tight to be used for flowers.

Small medallions of saints and martyrs are also made at Compton in the same manner, being painted in bright colours on a grey biscuit foundation. In this case, of course, the porous nature of the ware does not matter.

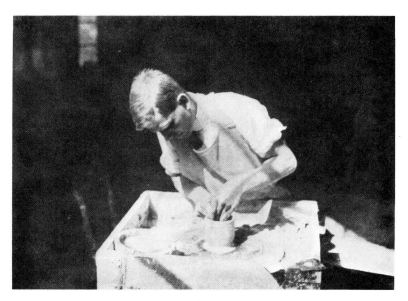

THE POTTER'S WHEEL

THE OUTPUT

THE COMPTON POTTERY

A great deal of the Devonshire ware is decorated before the first firing with ' slip '—clay in a creamy state—put on with a brush. The usual type of Aller Vale ware has a kind of incised decoration made by coating the body of red clay with white slip and scratching mottoes or designs in the outer coating so that the darker body shows through. Another favourite form of decoration is a picture of ships at sea made with. washes of coloured clay. This is known as ' Scandy ', from a Scandinavian who introduced it some thirty years ago. Grotesques are also made from designs of the same date.

The Barum ware relies for its effect mainly upon shape and colour. The larger pottery at Barnstaple has been in the hands of the same family for several generations and was well known some sixty years ago, when Devon pottery began to attract attention, for its ' coloured glazes and flowing and pulsating lines '.[1] Even before that date it had been staged at the Great Exhibition of 1851.

The firm at Rye is an example of an industry which continues to do a good trade in characteristic local ware of a rather old-fashioned type. Brown glazed bowls and jars decorated with heavy bunches of flowering hops in green and yellow, or with green wheat ears, have been amongst its products since 1882. There is also the ' Sussex pig ' with its inscription ' Won't be druv '. It divides into two parts, both head and body forming beer tankards, so that a man can truly say he has drunk ' a hogshead ' of beer. This pottery also makes plain blue and green vases and bowls, and others with glazes of shot colouring, and some less meritorious curiosities, such as baskets of plaited clay and modelled clay pails and shoes.

Many of the potteries which make vases and other decorative ware also keep up a steady production of plain household ware, the trade in which is less liable to fluctuation. The close connexion of decorative work with the purely utilitarian pottery is valuable from an aesthetic point of view, for the traditional shapes—beautiful in their fitness for purpose— of the kitchen bowls and jugs influence the potter towards simplicity in what he is apt to distinguish as ' art work '.

Glaze for pottery is called in Devonshire ' glass ', and is actually glass with other ingredients in it to make it fuse into the clay and colour it. This fusion of all the component parts is the essence of pottery, and it is the absence of it in the

[1] Professor Church, in a Lecture to the Society of Arts, quoted in *The Potter's Art in Devonshire*, J. Phillips. Devonshire Society, vol. xiii, 1881.

Potters' Art Guild ware which gives rise to condemnation from other potters. The potteries in the Torquay district make their own glaze, as do also those at Barnstaple, where both bright and dark glazes are produced. Many small potteries buy their glaze ready made, not considering it worth while to make it unless particular effects are desired. Experience and some knowledge of chemistry are necessary in order to obtain original effects with success. The outstanding feature of the Dicker pottery, in Sussex, is the use of special glazes, the secret of which is carefully preserved. The Deal pottery prides itself on a very beautiful blue glaze, which easily goes wrong with the slightest change of the clay used for the body. The vases made in a branch of the encaustic tile works at Poole are covered with glazes remarkable for beauty not only of colouring but also of surface, which look particularly well in company with flowers.

The proportion of unskilled labour to throwers needed in a small pottery varies according to the nature and scale of the output. In many cases the men vary their work a good deal—sometimes even the throwers must be called in to help pack the kiln and even to stoke it.

At the Waltham Abbey flower-pot works about twenty-six men are employed, four of whom are throwers. Amongst the ten men employed at Sheepfolds there were three throwers in 1922, all of them elderly. The best thrower was earning £4 10s. weekly, the men making the largest pots being paid most highly. The girls who work with the throwers, manipulating the clay and handing it to them, could earn up to 28s. a week (as compared with a pre-war 14s.) ; they are paid according to the men for whom they work, the better throwers needing more skilled and quicker girls. The wages paid here, in an industrial district, may not be indicative of the rates current in the rural south-western counties, which are certainly lower than those current in Staffordshire. (See below, page 147.)

At Burton-in-Lonsdale twenty men were employed in 1922, four skilled throwers among them. There were no apprentices, but one or two of the throwers were young men, not long out of their apprenticeship. It was easy at that time to get workers, as the closing of the Ingleton collieries made labour plentiful. The work of the Verwood pottery is carried on by eight men, including the proprietor, who superintends the business and teaches the learners. A small pottery in Truro employs only three men, one being a thrower, and two boys, one of whom turns the wheel. The Wattisfield pottery is owned by two brothers, one of whom works at the wheel. The other workers comprise an old man (also a skilled thrower), two younger men, and a boy to turn the wheel. One of the West Country firms is owned by two partners, one of whom, a thrower, works in the pottery, whilst the other, a painter, superintends unskilled workers in the decorating shed.

Several of the larger Devonshire potteries making Barum and Aller Vale ware employ from forty to sixty workers. In the South Devon potteries varying types of organization are to be found, from the small old-fashioned works where boys and girls are employed to turn the potters' wheels to the larger ones furnished with a quantity of modern machinery. Some of the latter seem to be at an awkward stage of development—still depending upon hand work for the most important processes and, indeed, not large enough to carry out mass production economically, and yet too large for the craftsman to have full scope for his powers.

A man can throw about two hundred and eighty large flower-pots—fifteen inches high—in a day, or one thousand of the smallest size (about three inches across the top). A very good thrower has been known to make fourteen hundred of the latter in a nine-hour day. Of large heavy meat pots, holding about a bushel, the potter makes forty in a day.

In the pottery industry, as in many others, there is a certain amount of controversy and disagreement concerning the time which should be served in apprenticeship. The traditional seven years is still advocated by several firms, but it is difficult to find boys willing to serve for so long a period with nominal wages. Before the war, boys began work at the Aller Vale pottery for 3s. 6d. or 4s. a week, with little advance in wages for some time. For flower-pot making, five or six years' training is generally considered by the older generation to be necessary for proficiency in making pots of all sizes up to the largest. At the Waltham Abbey works in 1923 one of the four throwers was a boy of seventeen who had been working for two or three years but could as yet only make the smaller pots.

The old throwers who served the full period of apprenticeship are proud of their skill and somewhat scornful of the younger generation of craftsmen. A good thrower is an artist of a high order and some of the most beautiful pottery is made where the thrower himself is the designer. There is more scope for a thrower in the small potteries of the southern counties than in industrial Staffordshire.

3203.2   L

Some small potteries with little variety in their output were, when visited, being carried on successfully by the labour of boys and girls under the supervision and training of one or two skilled craftsmen, with unskilled men to prepare the material and another man engaged to attend to the kiln when a batch was ready for firing. One boy thrower in a Dorset pottery in which scented ware was made was said to be skilful in making some dozen different shapes after only a fortnight's training and a few weeks' practice. A craftsman who is to produce flower-pots or brown kitchen ware, in which good workmanship and durability are of the utmost importance, would certainly need a longer training. The scented ware which was made so extensively in the Dorset potteries in 1921 was then enjoying a popularity which could hardly be long-lived and it is doubtful whether the training and experience of the boys and girls employed to make it would be of much use to them when the decline of this vogue should make it necessary for them to turn to work of a different type. The old-fashioned craftsman would be able after his seven years' apprenticeship to adapt his skill to making any kind of pot.

Undoubtedly there is in most girls and boys a good deal of latent talent which can easily, under good training, be turned to account in pottery work and which is most easily developed in youth. Girls are employed to decorate the beautiful ware made at Poole and in many other instances they have been found to be not only deft and quick with the brush but capable of really good original decorative work. A difficulty about the training of boys and girls in pottery—as in other—work is that when once they attain to proficiency in one branch of the craft—the making of a pot of one particular size and shape—they often prefer to concentrate on that in order to increase their speed and earn more money, rather than to continue their training and to become all-round craftsmen. The latter course, whilst causing them to earn less during their time of apprenticeship, will fit them to earn a better and more certain livelihood in later life. Some employers have been met with who, impatient of this short-sighted view in some of the boys they have taken into their works, have given up any attempt to train them and have condemned the younger generation in sweeping terms. On the other hand, the fault sometimes lies with the employers, who, finding that it serves their purpose well enough to employ a number of boys or young men who are able to make one or two kinds of pottery passably well, take no trouble to train them further. The difficulty can only be overcome by the master craftsmen themselves ; a good teacher, a man who takes a deep interest in his craft and has faith in his pupils, can arouse in them an enthusiasm for the details of the work and a willingness to learn which will help them to become skilled workers in their time.

Many of the workers in the larger potteries of Devonshire are organized with the Staffordshire pottery workers. Wages in Devon are below the Staffordshire rates and there is a general opinion that they will remain so. In so far as there is any competition between the Devonshire industry and that of Staffordshire the former, already handicapped by its remoteness, would probably be knocked out of the running if it had to pay the same rate of wages as its rival. Moreover, the cost of living is of course lower in Devon. The future prospects of the West Country potteries, however, seem to depend rather on their ability to produce distinctive hand-thrown ware than on their success in direct competition with factory products.

iv. *The Marketing of Pottery.*

The way in which the output of a pottery is marketed depends upon the kind of ware produced. Where household crocks—bread pans, meat jars, pitchers, and bowls—are made by a small rural firm the market for them is a local one. The Truro and Wattisfield potteries, for example, deliver their ware by motor-vans to retailers in towns within a radius of some thirty miles. In this way much expense is avoided. Not only is railway carriage dear, but when goods are sent in this way there is the additional carriage from the railway station to their destination. The goods have to be specially packed to travel by rail and, moreover, there is less risk of breakage when they are sent by van all the way, as they are only handled by the firm's own employees, who understand the special care needed. The rural pottery is enabled in this way to find a good market in its own immediate locality in spite of the competition of the larger industrialized firms of Staffordshire, many of which produce household ware of a similar kind, usually somewhat inferior in quality, and cheaper in price owing to the economy of mass production. These goods are sent by rail to all parts of the country. In one case it was said that, although the meat pots made by a rural firm cost in the first instance 6*d.*

a gross more than those from Staffordshire, yet the local makers could sell all their output without difficulty in the neighbouring towns, to which they could deliver the ware by van. Another example of a local market for this kind of ware is found in the north of England, where the bread mugs (large covered jars bulging in the middle, rather similar to meat pots), made at Wetheriggs, are sold in Penrith, Kendal, and a few towns in Scotland.

The most primitive method of marketing was found at Verwood, where the household ware is hawked about the countryside together with the besoms which are another local product. This Verwood firm and several others which produce both kitchen crocks and also ' fancy lines '—vases and other decorated ware—use two different methods of marketing. Whilst the heavier and simpler goods are sold locally—at the cottages and farmhouses in the Verwood district—the lighter things are sent by rail to retailers in more distant places. This is the case with the output of the Truro and Dicker potteries, and when some distinctive ware is produced, such as the Dicker ware, it may, once it has gained recognition, be sold to retailers all over England. The difficulty in this case is for a new maker to get his name known. The showing of the ware at handicraft exhibitions is useful and may lead to orders from new sources. The Potters' Art Guild sells much of its output through exhibitions, the medallions and smaller vases—costing from 2s. 6d. to 6s.—finding a ready sale. The ordinary commercial travellers seem to be of little use in the case of new and original work, although some type of ware which takes the popular fancy and is cheap, such as the scented vases made in several Devon potteries, may be disposed of successfully through this medium, even though the work is of poor quality. Quantities of scented ware were sold in 1921 to retailers at sea-side resorts and large orders for it were received from the colonies. Certain rural potters of a very different type from those who produce the scented ware, namely the flower-pot makers, also find a general rather than a local market for their goods, supplying retailers all over England.

A stoneware industry in the remote village of Burton-in-Lonsdale (Yorkshire), which is on a comparatively small scale—it employs some twenty men—has half a dozen horses and carts continuously in use carting the output, two thousand to three thousand spirit and jam jars and stew dishes weekly, to the station three miles away and carting back from it the ninety tons of coal used monthly. From the station the goods have to be sent by rail to the retailers, who comprise, so the manager declared, a 'world-wide' market. In spite of its disadvantageous situation, this firm seemed to be in a flourishing condition and it was said that the superiority of hand-thrown ware (such as that made here) over the 'jollied' ware of the industrial factories was universally recognized, and that the former could always command a better price and find a ready market, meeting with hardly any competition from ware of similar quality. Certainly this was the only rural pottery visited which specialized in these particular goods. It is the sole survivor of four potteries which existed in the village, the others having failed within the last twenty years. The failure of two of them is put down to the fact that they 'cut one another's throats', competing to reduce prices, whilst the third was given up owing to the difficulty of obtaining labour during the war.

v. *Character and Development of Small Rural Potteries.*

The small rural potteries can be roughly classified as the flower-pot firms, those making household ware, and those producing decorative pottery or what are called in the trade 'art goods'. In many cases the two latter types of output are combined. The flower-pot making is often a branch of brick, tile, and drain-pipe making, but as these latter industries have not been included in this survey, only the part of the business dealing with flower-pots need be considered. The actual making of these is more akin to other pottery work than to brick-making but often a similar clay is used for the pots to that which is used for bricks, and so the two are conveniently manufactured side by side.

On the whole there seems to be a steady prospect for the few flower-pot firms which exist, at least until some satisfactory method of making the pots by machinery is discovered. In some cases flower-pot making is combined with the production of other kinds of pottery. A certain proportion of the clay used in most flower-pot works is probably suitable for making pottery of a simple and rather heavy kind, such as household ware, and there might in some cases be a possibility of developing this industry side by side with the other. A thrower who is already skilled in making flower-pots of all sizes should be able, with little further training, to produce other shapes.

The branch of the rural pottery industry dealing with household ware has, however, declined considerably during the last twenty years. The firm at Truro is the sole survivor of eighteen formerly at work in Cornwall, all producing kitchen crocks for local sale, and that at Verwood is the only one left of eight which used to exist there. In other districts several were heard of as having died out within the last ten years or so. To some extent this decline is due to the competition of the large firms of Staffordshire and other industrial districts, which send their wares far and wide, but it has been shown that a small rural pottery can, by its method of distribution, meet competition successfully within its own immediate neighbourhood. The competition of cheap enamel ware, which has replaced pottery for so many household uses, must also be taken into account. Another factor is the gradual change in economic conditions and in house-keeping. Much of the household work in which pottery was used has been eliminated. The establishment of bakeries which send their vans into the remotest villages is responsible for the cessation of the demand for the Yorkshire ' punks ', the great pans in which bread was baked at home, and the use of separators has caused housewives to dispense with the big bowls in which milk stood for the cream to rise. Many other types of dairy and kitchen crocks are rapidly going out of common use and there is no chance of any considerable revival of demand for them. The very large pottery bowls and jars must always be costly since they are difficult to make and heavy and awkward to transport, and where some kind of big vessel is still needed, enamel ware often proves to be a cheaper substitute and is lighter and therefore easier to handle, whilst there is no danger of breakage.

There has been within recent years a certain trend of taste towards what is sometimes called the ' country cottage ' style in pottery, as in furniture. Toilet ware and jugs, and jars and bowls for the table, made in simple shapes, often modelled on the traditional patterns for household ware, have achieved a good deal of popularity. This type of ware is usually rather thick and heavy. Some jugs and bowls are only glazed inside, but other articles are covered with glazes in very beautiful colourings. The firms which make the old-fashioned bread pans, meat pots, milk bowls, and similar things are fitted for the production of this ' cottage ware ', and when the trade in the former shows signs of decline they might well turn their attention to varieties of coloured glazes and to new shapes and thus develop the industry in a direction which seems to offer good prospects. When any change of this kind is made in the output of a pottery the question of marketing has to be considered. New wares may mean new customers and these may have to be reached through new channels. A dealer who understood both the limitations and the capabilities of small rural firms and had a genuine interest in their development could do much to help them. This is one of the many cases in which co-operation between workers in the modern arts and crafts movement and the village craftsmen of the old tradition may be helpful to both. Organizations such as the Rural Industries Bureau and the Country Industries Trading Society, as well as the various handicraft associations which organize exhibitions of work, can help the older country firms to find new markets, can advise them as to modern demands, and can put them in touch with sources of technical knowledge. The newcomer amongst village craftsmen can, in his turn, learn much from the man whose handiwork carries on an unbroken tradition from the medieval craft-workers.

The potteries in the south-western counties which were turning out the scented ware for which there was a vogue in 1921 were in the anomalous position of small rural firms prospering by the mass production of cheap goods which were popular not because of, but in spite of, being hand-thrown. The hand processes had been simplified to such an extent that the semi-skilled work needed could be carried out by boys who were quickly trained. It is not often that a small firm far from an industrial district can compete successfully in work of this kind with the large firms of Staffordshire, and it is hardly likely that they have much chance of future development along these lines. This ware was sold through the ordinary commercial middlemen, who would encourage a firm to produce any article for which there is a large demand, even if the demand is only a temporary one, for their interest in the industry only depends upon the profit they can make from it. Some of these firms which produced scented ware, anticipating a slump when the fashion should die out, were preparing to produce glazed ware of other types, and at least one of them intended to make glaze in its own works. The most hopeful feature of these potteries was that, being themselves a new departure, they were in the hands of men ever on the outlook for new ideas, who, if they were to study better models—

both old and modern work—and concentrate on producing the kind of ware for which the local clay and the organization of a small rural firm are best suited, might become an important new force in the industry.

In some of the Devon potteries the difficulties of a stage of development between that of the small rural firm and the larger one organized on factory lines were illustrated. When machinery is introduced it is often necessary to increase the output in order to utilize the power economically. There is then a danger that the character of the work may be lost. In some cases one firm had copied the work of another and they then entered into competition to reduce prices, with the result that the standard of workmanship was lowered and the output began to approximate to the cheaper kinds of factory ware.

The small potteries are more likely to prosper by developing to the utmost their special characteristics—those which distinguish them from the larger industrial firms. Personal contact between the master craftsman and all the workers should be one of these points and it is one which helps to give distinction and individuality to the work and methods. Some of the West Country firms invite visitors to their workshops as a means of advertisement and thus carry on a certain amount of direct retail trade. Though this practice has been resented in some quarters as encroaching on the rights of the wholesaler, it succeeds in its object of arousing the interest of the public and is particularly useful in industries carried on near to pleasure resorts. For most people anything which they have seen in course of manufacture has an added attraction, and small rural potteries might well exploit this fact to a greater extent.

Another advantage enjoyed by any small rural firm is that experimental work is very easily carried out. Where the proportion of highly skilled workers is a large one and there is scope for the exercise of individual talent, it is not difficult to vary the output and to try new shapes or new glazes. This should be valuable in keeping the work alive and in preventing it from sinking into the rut of a too rigid routine. The existence of small enterprises carried on by artists may have a stimulating influence upon other potteries in the vicinity.

The fundamental difference between the rural potteries and the large firms of the industrial districts is that the whole organization of the former centres around their use of local clay and its treatment by the thrower, while the others, having chosen proximity to their fuel rather than to their raw material, send for the latter to Cornwall and to places beyond the seas, and much of their art consists in the skilful blending of different ingredients.

Hand-throwing, the other essential point which distinguishes the rural from the larger firms, is perhaps the key to the future development of the country potteries. This process is now practically extinct in the Staffordshire firms, and some throwers from the Midlands, having been superseded there by machines, have come south to Devon, where the craftsman can still find opportunity for individual work. The factory product is designed in the light of great technical knowledge concerning ' bodies ' and glazes and the action of firing upon them ; it is carried out by the executive skill of perhaps dozens of workers, who are merely ' hands ' working under exact direction. The part played by the chemist is as important as that played by the artist and, except in the case of a few special pieces of ware produced not for the ordinary market but for connoisseurs, the part played by actual workers is almost mechanical, machinery being utilized to the greatest possible extent. In the rural pottery, on the other hand, a great deal depends upon the thrower, particularly upon his ability to make his pots as light as possible without any sacrifice of strength and to finish the shaping of the pot whilst it is on the wheel, dispensing with turning or any other ' fettling ' process which would weaken the pot and destroy its character and which also involves additional expense. In many cases the thrower himself is the designer. He is often unconscious of any artistic merit in his work. He knows that it is good of its kind and serves its purpose, but ' art ' is not a word that he connects with good workmanship. He himself would class as ' art goods ' anything for an ornamental purpose and which is decorated in any way—even the unglazed scented pots with paper coats of arms gummed on to them and covered with varnish—but not the simple pitchers and bowls which are often the outcome of a much higher grade of craftsmanship. Students from the art school often go to watch the Truro thrower at his work, but he thought that their interest in it was merely due to the fact that it was ' old fashioned '.

When the designer has a good sense of form and colour, work of high quality can often be produced by the simplest means. But the system of organization in the small potteries makes success dependent upon the skill of all the workers and first of all upon that of the thrower, the chief craftsman. There is at present a shortage of throwers, and at the same

time there are a number of only semi-skilled boys and girls
engaged in the industry, particularly in the south-western
counties. The whole question of training is an important
one. A worker in a small firm needs not only to be skilled
in one process but at least to understand something of the
whole course of manufacture from the preparation of the
clay to the firing of the kiln. Where the number of workers
is small it may often be necessary for a man to turn his hand
to some other job than his own. In any case it is important
that, as the chief craftsmen grow old, some younger men
should be trained by them and be ready to take their places
in due course, for so much depends upon each worker and
so little of the work is purely routine. The controller of
the work—who is often both owner and master-craftsman—
can only carry out his ideas adequately if all his men put not
only their skill but their keen interest into the industry. If
the manager pays too little attention to the training of the
workers and concentrates all knowledge in himself, the
method of production is bound to develop on industrial
lines, thus bringing the firm into unequal competition with
large factories.

Art schools in Devon provide some opportunities for
training in decorative work, but the potters themselves were
inclined to condemn the teaching as unsuitable. In one
case it was said that china painting was taught which was
unrelated to work done in the local potteries. Another
criticism was that, in one school, colour and design were
sacrificed to mere quickness and deftness with the brush.
Some potters, however, spoke with appreciation of the classes.
There seems to be need for closer co-ordination of the teaching with the work done by local firms, and the effects of
training will be short-lived unless students are taught not
merely to copy, but to design for themselves and to understand the relation between the finished article and the raw
material of which it is made. The manager of a Sussex
pottery not only studies for himself the shape and colouring
of museum specimens, but endeavours to widen the educational value of his work by inviting schools in the neighbourhood to bring parties of children round the works.

The future success of the small rural firms must depend
upon the recognition, not only by the actual directors of
and workers in the industry, but by all who are concerned
with it, as teachers, dealers, or customers, of its essential
difference from the Staffordshire industry. If each works
along its own lines the question of competition will not arise.

vi. *Glass Making*.

The manufacture of glass usually reaches too large a scale to be considered rural, but some experiments in Cornwall and Devon have been investigated on account of their comparatively small scale and local character.

Before the war a Yorkshire man opened glass works at Hayle, near St. Ives (Cornwall), which were closed down during the war but reopened in 1921, and it chanced that a visit was paid to them on the very day that the first bottles were made. The raw material at the moment consisted of all the broken bottles which could be got from chemists, and amongst the local chemists the firm hoped to find its market. It was expected that later on the sand of the neighbourhood, which is near the sea, would be utilized in making black glass for beer bottles.

In bottle making a small lump of molten glass from the furnace is taken up at the end of a long tube through which the worker blows, thus hollowing out the glass as it begins to harden. The outer contour is given by pressing the bottle into a mould while the glass is still soft. Great skill is needed to carry out the whole process while the glass, which hardens rapidly, is in a malleable condition. Even in 1921 boys were being trained to blow the glass, and the employer said that these boys would soon earn £3 a week. It was expected that before long there would be as many as fifty workers of all sorts. Three hundred gross of bottles could be turned out from the furnace. At a time when numbers of lads were emigrating from Cornwall owing to the depression of the mining industry this new enterprise was opportune.

The Glass Makers' Trade Union had agreed to let the venture be independent of union regulations for three years, after which time it was considered that the firm ought to be sufficiently prosperous to be able to conform to the usual regulations regarding hours and wages which are made for the benefit of the employees.

At Meldon, near Okehampton (Devon), there is rock from which glass is made which is said to be the strongest in the world. The glass is green, black, and amethyst, none that is quite colourless having yet been produced. When the district was visited water-power was being harnessed to work a mill for grinding the rock to powder for making the glass. The stone must be heated to thirteen hundred degrees Centigrade to make it fuse, and gas from tar and compressed air heats the furnace for it. The manager was hopeful that peat gas might become available from the Duchy peat set near Bridestowe, not many miles away. The Duchy of Cornwall grants the right to quarry the stone, and there had been no trouble from commoners of Dartmoor.

In order to teach the English workers, some Belgians and Austrians had been employed. In 1921 there were about fifty workers, mostly boys, who earned from 27s. to 30s. a week. This was a few shillings more than the district rate for boys, the higher amount being given to make up for the long walk from Okehampton, where they all lived. Great skill in throwing can sometimes be discovered among the workers and it provides scope for subsidiary arts at these glass factories.

CHAPTER VI

LAPIDARY WORKERS

Jet and Serpentine Cutters.

THE two small workshop industries of making ornaments
from jet and serpentine are somewhat similar in character.
Both use a local material mined in the neighbourhood and
in both cases the material is worked up by hand into trinkets
and other small articles which are sold to visitors in the
districts where the material is found, although the worked
jet is also sold to dealers for retail elsewhere.

In the British Isles jet is mined only in the Whitby cliffs,
where it has been worked for many hundreds of years—in
fact it is said that the Phoenicians who came to England to
trade with the ancient Britons used to ' barter beads for
Whitby jet '. A certain amount of Spanish jet—which is
declared by the Whitby craftsmen to be of inferior quality
—is imported in the rough state to be worked up in London.
Except for this, Whitby supplies English towns and many
foreign countries with all the jet for which they have a market.

The mines at Whitby run inland from the face of the cliff,
the jet being found in seams, as coal is. It is only mined now
by individuals working independently, who generally have
an agreement with the owner of the property to give him
a quarter of the proceeds. If a new mine is opened and
nothing is discovered the miner pays nothing. There is
no indication of any failure of the supply.

The methods of working up the jet have remained practically the same through at least four or five generations.
The introduction, by the largest firm, of motor power to turn
the wheels is the only innovation. Carving is done by means
of a knife with a tiny blade, forged by a local smith ; it has
to be specially tempered for cutting jet and the smith must
understand exactly what is required. Jet which is to be
worked on the grindstone is first ' blocked up ' with a chisel
from the rough lumps. Beads are turned on the lathe, being
shaped with a chisel, and then drilled. The facets of the
beads or other ornaments are next ' roughed out ' on the
grindstone—the stone for which may be found on the beach
and requires only to be dressed by a mason. The lead-mill

is next used, this being a wheel which removes the coarse
marks of the grindstone.   Then the jet is polished on a
' polishing wheel ' or ' wood board ', a revolving wooden wheel
rubbed with rotten-stone.   Another polishing wheel, with
cloth sides, is also used, and a brush.   Incised patterns are
made with the cutting wheel, which has a steel blade edge.
This has to be tempered so that it will cut glass before it
will cut jet, which is very hard.   Some attempts are said to
have been made to manufacture a substitute for jet, but no
substance of the same quality and hardness has been produced.
     The miners sell the raw jet in rough lumps to the jet
ornament makers.   A number of the latter are old men, with
their own tools and workshops, who work as their own
masters.   In addition to these there are seven shops, each
with its own workroom employing two or three men.   There
is also one manufacturer on a larger scale who employs in
his workshop eleven men, one boy, and three girls to thread
beads and join up bracelets and so forth.   The older men
are generally skilled carvers as well as workers with the wheel,
and served their apprenticeship, some of four or five years,
some of seven.   Although the industry is prosperous there
seem to be very few young workers or learners.   Only one
apprentice—in the largest workshop—was discovered.   Large
carved cameos and flower brooches used to be very popular,
and the carving of these was very skilled work, in fact a man
had to have some special aptitude if he were to become very
good at it.   The present demand is chiefly for faceted beads,
bracelets, and brooches, cut out on the grindstone and lead-
mill, and this work can be quickly learned.
     Skilled men were earning 1s. 6d. an hour in 1922 and the
apprentice received £1 a week and had one hour's instruction
each evening ;   during the day he was employed on more or
less unskilled work.   The apprentice had been working for
eleven months and was described as ' already getting handy '.
Men who are trained turners or cabinet-makers sometimes
take up jet working and find it easy.
     Jet workers sell their produce in summer to the local shops,
which rely chiefly on the custom of the summer visitors,
some being closed in winter.   In the winter the worked
jet is sold to dealers in London, Birmingham, and other
towns.   The one manufacturer whose business is organized
on a comparatively large scale works entirely for export,
three-quarters of his produce going to America, both North
and South, and the rest to South Africa and other countries.
     There are said to have been fifteen hundred workers in

the industry only fifty years ago, and even fifteen years ago
there were still about twenty shops, but of these only seven
have survived. During the last ten years, however, the
industry has steadily improved and the still existing shops
are said to be far more flourishing than the twenty ever
were, for the extension of the export trade has restored
prosperity to the industry.

Serpentine occurs in Cornwall, near the Lizard. It varies
in colour, some pieces being reddish, others green and others
grey with veins of vivid green and pink. This industry is
of much more recent origin than jet working, the possibilities
latent in serpentine having been first perceived by the
Prince Consort, by whose suggestion and encouragement the
industry of cutting, polishing, and setting the stone was
developed. It is reported that the larger pieces of serpentine
are now becoming rarer, although quantities of the smaller
ones are still to be found. In some places small pieces of the
stone can be taken away free of charge, but as a rule the
stone-cutters have to pay for what they take.

The industry is carried on chiefly by independent workers,
but in Helston there are a few men employed by a firm. The
total number of cutters at work at the Lizard and in Helston
is not more than about a dozen. In Penzance one cutter was
seen at work behind a jeweller's shop, and the work has also
been done at St. Ives, but the stone is heavy to transport
and is more economically worked up near the quarries.

Serpentine is cut, shaped, and polished on a treadle lathe.
No power machinery is used and it is said that, although
with the larger pieces the treadle lathe involves hard work,
the method is satisfactory. The objects made are models
of the Eddystone Lighthouse, vases, inkpots, letter-weights,
buttons, tiny barrels containing minute photographs of local
views with a lens to magnify them, ' Cornish pasties ' to wear
on a chain, and other ornaments. The workers are guided
in what they make by the size and shape of the pieces of
raw stone on which they work. Most of the work is sold
direct to the public by the workers, who show it in little
glass-fronted sheds, many of them attached to the workshops. The chief sale is among visitors who come to the
district in the summer and like to take home the serpentine
ornaments as souvenirs. During the winter the men are
kept busy re-stocking their shops for the summer season.

A similar weakness is inherent in both the jet and serpentine
industries. Though the workmanship is skilled the taste in
which it is carried out is not of a high order. The hat-pins,

brooches, and buttons made by the serpentine workers are cemented on to cheap brass or tin mounts bought by the gross from Birmingham. These detract from the artistic value of what is made and result in trinkets of the type which are sold in cheap fancy shops. The industry has been exploited by a Birmingham ' stone-cutting ' firm which supplies shops of this class. Serpentine needs very little setting but its beauty would be enhanced if it were set in silver, copper, or bronze, according to whether the prevailing colour in the stone were grey, green, or red. As regards jet, the simple faceted beads represent probably the most satisfactory method of working up this material but a great many commonplace ornaments are also made, and poorly mounted, for sale in cheap jewellery shops. The chief merit at present in the work both in jet and in serpentine is that it is done by hand and the men are well-trained and skilled.

APPENDIX

THE BRANDON FLINT KNAPPERS

An industry which is probably the oldest in the British Isles and is of interest chiefly for that reason, still exists at Brandon, on the borders of Norfolk and Suffolk. This is flint knapping, which is carried on in much the same way to-day as in the neolithic age, although in the course of time the flints have been prepared for many different purposes. About three miles from Ling Heath, where the flints are now dug, are the circular shafts known as Grimes' Graves, from which the prehistoric men dug their flints to be made into arrow-heads, knives, and fish-hooks. After the use of iron became general for weapons and edged tools, flints were still used for tinder lighters, and it is probable that the working of them never stopped. In 1686 flint locks were introduced into the British Army and the flint knapping industry became an important one and flourished until 1835, when flints were superseded by percussion caps. Since that time the industry has gradually declined, but there is still a certain demand for gun flints for use in the old-fashioned fire-arms which are supplied to the natives of West Africa and the Gold Coast, who must be armed so that they may shoot game but whom it is politic to arm less efficiently than the representatives of the ruling race.

In 1868 there were thirty-six flint knappers at work, not including the stone diggers ; in 1878 the number had fallen to twenty-six, and there were ten diggers ; in 1923 there were only four men engaged in flint knapping, of whom at least one had an alternative occupation, and one old man digging the flints, who has been a digger since boyhood. There was a steady trade in gun flints until 1914, but the war caused an interruption. Some of the men were needed for other work and, although they have since returned to their industry, it is in a flagging condition and the workers gave it as their opinion that it will probably die out.

The work of the flint knappers is described in detail in the monograph written by Mr. S. B. J. Skertchly in 1879. He shows that their tools and methods are based on those of their prehistoric forerunners, whereas the methods of the French knappers, who were at work until recently, show a complete break with tradition. The one-sided pick still used in England is a remarkable link with the neolithic man's tools, for it is simply a replica of the deer's antlers used by him. The French use an ordinary double-headed pick. The neolithic tool used for flaking was a smooth, oval pebble of quartz. Later, a slight notch was made on one or both sides to give a better grip, and later still holes were drilled through and a small handle inserted. The old English flaking hammer was identical in shape with this stone tool, but a French hammer is now used.

Flints have been knapped in modern times at Beer Head, in Devon, where a landslip on the cliffs disinterred a quantity of black flints ready to hand, and also at Glasgow, but the Brandon industry seems to be the only one now surviving.

Ling Heath, where the flints are dug, is a common about one hundred and sixty acres in extent, held in trust for the poor of the village of Brandon a couple of miles away. The heath is let by auction every seven years and is usually leased for the sake of the game by the owner of one of the neighbouring estates. The lessee charges a groundage of 1s. 10d. for each ' jag ' or cartload of flints which is taken away. A jag has been variously described as being about half a ton or one ton in weight. A jag which was weighed by Mr. Skertchly proved to be 13 cwt. 1 lb. Not more than fifty or sixty tons of flint are now removed annually. At one time there were elaborate unwritten laws as to digging rights, but now that only one digger is at work these have fallen into disuse.

The digger sinks a shaft from thirty to seventy feet in depth and brings up the big flints, as he finds them, on his head. There are three grades of flints—tops, walls, and floors—the first being of inferior quality. The flints are piled on the ground beside the shaft until a jag is collected, which is sold to the local flint knappers. Two days is the average time taken to bring up a jag, a pit yielding from two or three to four or five jags a week. The average time taken to sink a shaft thirty feet deep is three weeks. In 1923 a jag was sold for 15s., the buyer paying both groundage and carting.

After the flints have been dug there are four processes of manufacture—drying, quartering, flaking, and knapping. The flints are first dried before a fire to evaporate the moisture. The necessity for having them very dry makes the work unhealthy, the dusty particles which are thrown off in the other processes being inhaled by the workers.

In the quartering process the knobbly flint is held on the

QUARRYING THE FLINTS

QUARTERING

FLINT KNAPPING

worker's knee, placed so as to bring a flat or hollowed part into position for the quartering hammer. After a slight preliminary tapping a blow is given from the elbow, breaking the flint so as to leave an edge as square as possible from which to begin flaking. The next process, that of flaking, is the one which requires the most skill. It is the one process which is said to be carried out better to-day than in the neolithic age. As Mr. Skertchly says : ' The stone must be struck at the proper angle, in the exact spot, with a certain force, and on a given portion of the face, and all but the first of these elements vary with every flake.' The outer flakes struck from the flint, called ' shives ', which show the white coating, are waste. As these are removed the block takes on a roughly pyramidal form, from which the next series of flakes is cut. A perfect flake has a flat face, even edge, and parallel ribs all the way down.

The last process, that of knapping, from which the whole industry takes its name, is the actual making of the gun flints from the flakes. Four kinds of flints are now made, musket, carbine, horse pistol, and pocket pistol, which range from large to very small. The knapper takes the flake in his left hand, resting it on a small iron bar, and decides at a glance what kind of flint it will make. With the slender knapping hammer in his right hand he taps the flake repeatedly with a movement from the wrist, first cutting it across and then striking pieces off to shape the flint and trim the edges. The whole process is carried out very rapidly, the knapper seeming to turn the flint without ceasing, and yet each blow falls exactly where it is needed. The tapping of the hammer is kept up continuously, light blows falling on the worker's bench (which in one case was made from a tree stump) whilst he is picking up a fresh flake. It is possible to make several flints, sometimes four or five, from one flake, but in practice only one is usually made, because the pieces of the flake which are struck off fly in all directions and the time which would be spent in hunting for them would not be compensated for by the saving in flint. Although the knappers shape the flints with great accuracy and rapidity, authorities consider that modern workmanship in the knapping process is not to be compared with that of the neolithic man, whose even surface chipping of arrow-heads was a triumph of skill.

Jags vary not only in size but in quality, and the number of flints which can be made from one jag varies from eight thousand to twelve thousand. Mr. Skertchly mentions six thousand as the average number and says that a good jag has been known to yield eighteen thousand flints, including some of the smallest size. The finished flints represent only a very small proportion of the bulk of the raw material. For example, from the jag of thirteen hundredweight which Mr. Skertchly weighed, the total number of flints made (10,850) weighed only one hundredweight six stone.

The most skilful of the knappers now at work can make four hundred finished flints in an hour, but his speed was said to be exceptional. Another man makes from seven hundred to eight hundred flakes, or about three hundred flints, in the same time. Mr. Skertchly estimates the average number of flints made in a minute as eight, which, representing four hundred and eighty in an hour if the pace was kept up, would seem to indicate that the speed of the knappers at that time (1879) was greater than at present.

The flints may be sold to a middleman in Brandon at from 5s. to 6s. a thousand, according to quality, or direct to the gun manufacturers at from 9s. to 12s. a thousand. The advantage of selling to the middleman is that he will take the knapper's whole output, so that the latter is sure of a regular weekly income, whereas the orders received from the gun manufacturers are irregular, and the knapper may be unlucky enough to have a large stock of flints of one particular size left on his hands for some time when the demand is only for other sizes.

Supposing that a knapper spends eight hours a week on the preliminary work, he might then make some 9,750 flakes in thirteen hours and in another thirty-two and a half hours would make 9,750 flints from these flakes. Thus, his output in a week of fifty-three and a half hours might sell for about £2 8s. 9d. (a minimum price) to the middleman, or for as much as £4 17s. 6d. direct to the manufacturers, but from this must be deducted about £1 as the price of the jag, with groundage and carting.

There is, of course, no possibility of the revival or development of the flint knapping industry, which is already an anachronism and is doomed to die out in the natural course of events. Although the industry is of considerable interest as a link with prehistoric times, its extinction cannot be regretted from the point of view of social reform owing to the fact that the work tends to engender consumption and diseases of the throat and chest. It is said that most of the workers die from these causes. There does not seem to be any means of improving the conditions of the industry, for the flints can only be worked in a dry state and it is their dryness which causes the fine dust during the flaking and knapping processes, which permeates the whole workshop. The supply of flint lock rifles to the natives of Africa is hardly an end of sufficient importance to justify the continued employment of men in these unhealthy conditions.

Flint knapping is in no way related to any other rural industry except by the fact that a local cooper supports himself by making the kegs in which the flints are packed to send away.

INDEX